To the spirit of Halloween
and the fun it brings
to families everywhere

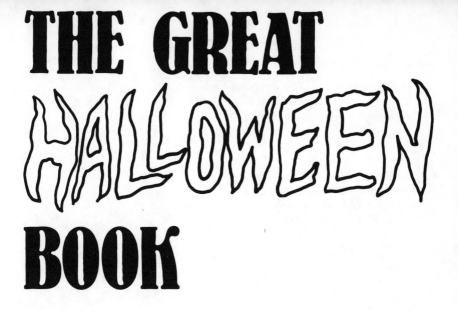

THE GREAT HALLOWEEN BOOK

Mark Walker

HOW TO MAKE THIS HOLIDAY MORE FUN FOR THE WHOLE FAMILY!

First printing: August, 1983
Second printing: August, 1984
Third printing: August, 1989

© Mark Walker, 1983
LIBERTY PUBLISHING COMPANY
Deerfield Beach, Florida

Published by:
Liberty Publishing Company, Inc.
440 South Federal Highway
Deerfield Beach, FL 33441

Library of Congress #82-84276
ISBN 0-89709-038-1

Manufactured USA

TABLE OF CONTENTS

HALLOWEEN

A crisp, clear October night. The whisper of dead leaves rustling mysteriously down the darkened streets. The smell of candy apples and freshly-carved pumpkins. And, most of all, an eerie parade of spectres, apparitions, monsters and goblins moving silently through the starless night to knock on the doors of brightly-lit houses.

Halloween is the most magical of times, the one night in the year when reality and illusion blend together in an enchanting aura of the supernatural. It is a night when anything seems to be possible, a time when anyone can assume any identity that he or she wants. Of all our holidays, Halloween offers the most possibilities for a short vacation from our everyday lives, and this book is meant to be a traveler's guide for that vacation. It includes tips for the trick-or-treater, suggestions for costumes that can be made inexpensively and easily at home, new and different ideas for Halloween parties for kids and adults alike, and much, much more. There is even a section on how to create your own haunted house.

But first, this chapter explains how it all began.

Halloween Throughout The Ages

The roots of Halloween can be traced back thousands of years to ancient Rome. Each October, the Romans celebrated the Feast of Pompona, the Goddess of Orchards. The observance of this holiday included bobbing for apples and the exchange of small gifts of fruit and nuts. The Romans also believed that protection from evil spirits could be gained by hollowing out gourds and placing a lit candle or oil-soaked rag inside.

The ancient Greeks believed that once a year the souls of the dead returned to visit the earth. Rather than offend these supernatural visitors, the Greeks held the week-long festival of Anthesteria, when banquets were given in honor of the dead, and their souls were "invited" to attend. Once the week was over though, the souls of the dead were sent back to the underworld by Greek priests who chanted: "Begone, ye ghosts: it is no longer Anthesteria."

While the Greeks and Romans were celebrating their festivals, the Celtic peoples of Western and Central Europe were also paying homage to the supernatural. The Celtic new year fell on November 1, and new year's eve was marked by the festival of Samhain, the Lord of Death. Celtic priests were called Druids, and these mysterious sorcerers commanded the people to light huge bonfires in which animals, and sometimes luckless humans, were sacrificed to appease the dreaded Samhain. The Celtic families let their household fires go out, and then lit a new one from the village bonfire to signify their hope for prosperity in the coming year.

The Roman invasion and conquest of the Celtic territories led eventually to a combination of the festivals of Samhain and Pompona, and the development of new traditions. Celtic children began to parade the streets in costumes during the Samhain vigil, and to participate in the apple-bobbing and gifts of fruits and nuts associated with the Roman feast of Pompona. Bonfires and sacrifices continued to be an important part of this pagan celebration, since the Celts believed that the dark lord Samhain caused the souls of the wicked to be reincarnated as animals, especially black cats, and no one was anxious to have these spooky creatures around.

The spread of Christianity throughout Europe eventually

reached the Celts, and the Christian missionaries were appalled at the pagan practices that took place at the end of each October. These traditions were so important to the Celts, however, that the missionaries realized that they could not be discarded altogether—or the missionaries themselves might end up in bonfires. The solution was to let the Celts hold onto their pagan customs, but to somehow turn the feast of Samhain into a Christian holiday. The church leaders decided to proclaim November 1 as All Hallow Day, a day to honor all the saints who did not already have a feast day of their own. The night before this became All Hallow Evening—later shortened to Halloween. Even though the Celtic people were eventually converted to Christianity the missionaries, try as they might, were never able to stamp out the pagan rituals of the Samhain vigil which later became the traditions of Halloween.

During the Middle Ages, people believed that Halloween was the night when Satan and the damned were released from hell to search for victims. The story went that if one of these evil spirits found someone committing even the smallest sin, and if that person were not protected by a wreath of garlic or a lit jack-o'-lantern, then the demon would enter the sinner's body and possess it forever. Naturally, most medieval Halloweens were spent huddled around home fires in prayer for protection against the devil and his evil hordes.

Different countries held different Halloween superstitions. In Wales it was thought that a sneeze on Halloween would momentarily release the soul from the body. If the devil was quick enough, he could snatch the soul and drag it away. This is why "God bless you" became the universal response to a sneeze. Scottish tradition says that each Halloween the devil appears in a kilt, playing a ghostly bagpipe.

In some Scottish villages, offerings of cakes were made to the goblins and witches thought to be on the prowl. The Scots also believed that the wood of the rowan tree was protection against evil spirits, and everyone made sure to carry a sprig of rowan on Halloween.

In England, Halloween was sometimes called Nutcrack Night or Snap-Apple night, and the holiday was more closely associated with the harvest season. English families would sit by the fire and tell each other spooky stories while they ate apples and nuts. The English also associate Halloween with their celebration of Guy Fawkes Day on November 5. This holiday commemorates the discovery of the Gunpowder Plot in 1605, in which Guy Fawkes was apprehended while trying to blow up the English Parliament, along with King James I. On Guy Fawkes Day English children dance through the streets carrying effigies of the "Guy," and begging for "a penny for the Guy." This practice continues to this day.

Halloween was not widely celebrated in the United States until the middle of the 19th Century when hundreds of thousands of Irish and Scottish immigrants came to America. The immigrants brought their Halloween traditions with them, and these practices quickly became a part of American culture. Most modern American Halloween traditions—jack-o'-lanterns, trick-or-treating, pranks and practical jokes—can be traced directly to Ireland.

In Anoka, Minnesota, known as "The Halloween Capital of the World," Halloween is a community-wide celebration which lasts for an entire week. There are activities and festivities for all ages, ranging from a costume contest for pre-schoolers to a wine-tasting party for adults. The youngsters in school are entertained by jugglers and comedians. On the Thursday or Friday preceeding Halloween, there is a Kids' Parade, with floats provided by local civic organizations and approximately 3,500 elementary students marching in costume.

On the Saturday nearest to Halloween, the main events take place. The Grand Day Parade, an annual tradition since 1921, lasts about 2½ hours and is witnessed by about 10,000 spectators. Over 200 floats and marching bands, some from as far as 100 miles away, regularly participate. The evening is capped by the finals of the Queen's Pageant, when one lucky contestant is crowned from among 35 entrants who participate in a number of events during the week, including style shows.

There are a number of other cities and towns throughout the United States where Halloween is a major occasion, but none where nearly every resident is involved.

Today the celebration of Halloween is primarily limited to the English-speaking world, and concentrated in Ireland, Canada and the United States. While some of the older traditions—such as elaborate and sometimes overly-mischievous practical jokes— are dying out, most Halloween activities remain remarkably faithful to their Celtic origins.

Photographs courtesy of *Anoka County Union*

TRICK-OR-TREAT

This chapter is devoted to the most traditional of Halloween customs—trick-or-treating. It includes information on the origins of this custom and the evolution to its present form. There is a section on safety tips, and some ideas on how to turn the tables by staying at home on Halloween and playing tricks on the ghostly visitors who come to your door. Finally, a list of inexpensive non-edible gifts is included as an alternative to the usual Halloween treats.

How Trick-or-Treating Began

Modern trick-or-treating has its origins among the Celtic peoples of Scotland, Wales, and especially Ireland. An ancient Celtic custom revolved around one of the Druid gods named Muck Olla. On the feast of Samhain, groups of peasants went from house to house demanding money and food in the name of Muck Olla. Those who gave generously were assured prosperity; those who didn't often became the victims of practical jokes and other mischief.

The Muck Olla tradition came to America with the Irish and Scottish immigrants in the 1840's. As years passed, youngsters came to consider Halloween as the one night of the year when adults would tolerate behavior that would not be permitted at other times.

Housewives began to offer candy, cookies and apples to children on Halloween in exchange for a promise to cut out the pranks and mischief. This practice eventually evolved into the tradition of "trick-or-treat."

Safety Tips

Trick-or-treating *must* be carefully supervised by adults. One positive aspect of the 1982 Tylenol scare was to emphasize the importance of adult supervision and safety precautions for trick-or-treating. This tragedy also made everyone aware of those deranged individuals who, for some unimaginable reason, like to hand out sabotaged "treats." The only explanation is that

these creatures are the 20th century version of the demons who were thought to walk the earth in medieval times. Also, since trick-or-treating involves young children on the streets after dark, they should all travel in groups led by one or more of their parents or an older brother or sister.

For safety's sake, below is a precautionary trick-or-treating checklist:

- Make-up is preferable to masks since it doesn't obscure vision. If a mask is worn, make sure the eye holes are sufficiently large. Masks should be removed before crossing the street.

- Costumes should be non-flammable and bright enough to be seen at night. Robes, gowns, etc. must be short enough so that they can't be tripped over.

- Stress to all trick-or-treaters, especially the older ones, that they are *not* to eat any treats before they've been checked. It's a good idea to feed trick-or-treaters a big meal before they go out. That way, they won't be as tempted to nibble.

- If possible, stay in the home neighborhood, and visit only the houses of people that are known.

- Children should trick-or-treat in the late afternoon or early evening. They should be instructed to stay on streets that are well lit and to cross only at corners, and never between parked cars or the middle of the street.

This list could go on and on. The best recipe for safe and happy trick-or-treating is common sense, caution and adult supervision.

Surprising Trick-or-Treaters

On Halloween night, it can be just as much fun to stay at home and pull some spooky stunts on trick-or-treaters rather than go out. The whole family can get into the act. In some neighborhoods, it is traditional for trick-or-treaters to go to a certain house on Halloween night where they *never* know what to expect.

Preparations for trick-or-treaters can be either simple or elaborate. One of the oldest stunts is to simply tape the latch on the door so that it's not really closed. When someone rings the bell, the door can be pulled open with a piece of strong thread attached to the inside doorknob. As the trick-or-treaters poke their heads into the dark room, switch an eerie green or orange light on before handing out the treats. Adults can also dress up to answer the door. A woman could be a witch, complete with a hat and broom. A man could use an old coat, add some fake shoulders and hidden eye holes, and answer the door as a headless man. Another idea is to fill a rubber glove with water and freeze it. Hold the frozen glove so that it sticks through the sleeve of an oversized coat, and give your trick-or-treaters a chill with a cold handshake. A vibrating hand buzzer will also result in a "thrilling" handshake.

A couple at home on Halloween can dress up as Mr. and Mrs. Frankenstein. Leaving the curtain to the front window open, they could rock away on rocking chairs as they wait for their trick-or-treaters. Another idea for couples is the "growing ghost." The woman answers the door and standing beside her is a sheet-covered ghost who suddenly begins to get taller. All the stunt requires is a plastic bowl, a long white sheet or cloth, and a five or six foot pole. The man, also covered by the sheet, holds the bowl on the pole in front of him. Slowly raising the pole creates the illusion of a growing ghost.

A family with a large yard can decorate it with cardboard headstones, so that the trick-or-treaters have to pass through a cemetery before they reach the house. Once there, they could be treated to a quick tour of a "mini" haunted house, which is really just one decorated room. The "mini" haunted house could include:

- A record or tape of weird music and horror sounds.
- Rubber bats and spiders manipulated by strong thread and a hidden assistant.
- Flashing lights, usually green or red.
- A bucket of dry ice and hot water to give off a fog effect. Make sure you place a screen over the top in order to prevent children from touching the ice.
- Spider webs—long pieces of black thread to dangle from doorways and brush against children's faces.
- A fake coffin made out of sheets of cardboard. At the conclusion of the tour, a person sits up inside the coffin and wishes everyone a Happy Halloween.

As the trick-or-treaters leave the house, give them a treat for their bravery.

A final suggestion for a family is the creation of "The Monster's House." Each trick-or-treater is admitted one at a time by the doorkeeper. As the child enters the house, he sees "The Monster" (appropriately costumed and made up) sitting perfectly still in a large chair. An old trunk sits at the Monster's feet. After a few seconds, the Monster beats his fist on the trunk three times. The trunk slowly opens, and a green arm emerges with a treat in its hand. The Monster motions the trick-or-treater to take the treat, and the hand slowly withdraws into the trunk. As the lid closes, the Monster points to the door. The child leaves, another is admitted, and the process is repeated. All that's needed for this stunt is the trunk, costume and mask for the Monster, and green make-up for the spooky hand of the child inside the trunk. Be sure the trunk has sufficient air holes and that hands and fingers are kept free of injury.

Alternative Treat Suggestions

Halloween treats need not be limited to candy. In fact, one way to take the worry out of Halloween for the trick-or-treaters' parents is to stay away from edible items entirely. Listed below are some inexpensive ideas for alternatives.

Shiny pennies or other coins
Halloween party favors
Fast food gift certificates
Small plastic bats or spiders
Toy rings or key chains
Baseball or Football cards
Colored pencils or pens
Grab bags
Talking bookmarks
T-Shirt transfers or patches
Commemorative stamps
Ghost Cards

Whether you or your children will be trick-or-treating, or going to a party, you'll need a costume. The next chapter contains suggestions for several "do-it-yourself" costumes that can be made easily and inexpensively.

HALLOWEEN COSTUMES

Costumes capture the true essence of Halloween. From the earliest days of the Druid Samhain festivals, people wore costumes to ward off the demons and ghosts that they believed to be roaming the earth on October 31. It was thought that if these supernatural visitors could not tell the living from the dead and demonic, they would be confused and return from whence they came.

Costumes and masks continued to be an integral part of the Halloween tradition through the years. As the custom of trick-or-treating developed, children and young adults began to wear costumes to "frighten" people into giving them treats, or to disguise themselves when playing Halloween pranks on their neighbors. Costumes continue to be a way for people to assume a different identity on Halloween night, and to use their ingenuity and imagination in so doing.

This chapter includes tips on both renting costumes and on designing and constructing home-made costumes easily and inexpensively. It should help to answer that age-old question, "What are you going to be for Halloween?"

Renting Costumes

There are thousands of costume shops around the world that rent costumes for Halloween and other special occasions. Before renting a Halloween costume, there are a number of important things to keep in mind.

First, don't wait until the last minute. Rental costumes have to be properly fitted and alterations are often necessary. The costumes will also have to be cleaned and pressed. All of this takes time, and it is advisable to arrange for a costume rental at least two or three weeks in advance. This also assures that a wide selection of costumes will still be available.

Rental prices can vary widely from shop to shop, so be sure to get the most for your money by comparing prices. Also inquire what the rental price includes, since some shops charge extra for accessories such as hats, boots, or capes. Finally, be certain of the shop's return policy, so that you're not charged for an extra day if the costume is brought back too late.

Renting is an easy way to come up with an elaborate costume quickly, but some individuals may find it too expensive. The rest of this chapter contains ideas for home-made costumes.

Do-It-Yourself Costumes

When most people decide to make their own Halloween costumes, they don't really have a clear idea of what they want the end result to be. That is why the best method is to decide exactly what the costume will look like in advance—sort of a "costume blueprint"—and then gather the materials needed to achieve that effect. This section contains several photographs and diagrams of home-made costumes, and provides the materials needed and the instructions for creating them.

Every household contains enough old clothes and related items to make numerous costumes. For men, items such as tuxedos, military uniforms, pants, shirts, vests, suits, and pajamas can all be used. Women's costumes can be made from gowns, formal dresses, blouses, underskirts, bathing suits and choir robes. Costumes for children can be created with sleeper pajamas, boxes, sheets and pillow cases, bags, and old adult clothing. If a certain article of clothing not available around the house is required for a costume, check with second-hand stores. They'll probably have the item at an affordable cost. If a different color is needed for, say, an old shirt, consider dyeing the material. Also, pieces of fancy trim, available from sewing or fabric shops, can be added to costumes to create the right effect.

After a home-made costume is completed it's sometimes effective to buy just one professional piece to add the final touch. For example, an authentic pirate hat would give a home-made pirate costume an aura of professionalism. Finally, be sure to carry at least one prop piece to complete the costume. A devil would carry a pitchfork, a gangster a violin case, or a caveman a club.

Box Costumes

Easy and inexpensive costumes especially for children can be made from cardboard and/ or cardboard boxes. After finding a suitably sized and shaped box, cut out holes to allow free movement of the head, arms and legs. Necessary additions to the box can be made with additional cardboard or other items and attached with glue, staples or sticky tape. Cover the box as required with paint, aluminum foil, contact paper, cloth or crepe paper. Below are listed a few box costume suggestions.

Robot

Cover the box with aluminum foil. Additions to the box could be made with bottle tops or other knobs and buttons to simulate the robot's dials and controls. Other additions to increase the effect could be painted on.

The arms and legs should also be covered with aluminum foil. Use an old pair of pants and a shirt and keep the foil in place with clear adhesive tape. Shoes could be covered with foil, or black boots worn. A pair of black rubber gloves make a good substitute for the robot's hands.

The robot's head could be represented by a mask or make-up, or another small cardboard box could be decorated to fit over the head.

Die

Cut the bottom from a square box long enough to extend from your neck to slightly above the knees. Cut a hole in the top, large enough to get your head through, plus two smaller ones in the sides for arms. Paint each outside panel (5 remaining) of the box with a different number of spots between 1 and 6.

A couple could dress up as a pair of dice. If so, they should wear green eye visors adorned with the words "Las Vegas." Red arm garters could also be used. Arms and legs should be covered with either a black leotard and tights, or black pants and a shirt.

Television

Cut the bottom from a large box, and a smaller square hole for the face. Cover the hole from the inside with transparent plastic, held in place by tape. Cover the entire box with wood grain contact paper or paint. Knobs and a rabbit ear's antenna could also be added.

Jack-In-The-Box

Cut the top and bottom out of a square box. Reinforce the box on the inside at the corners so that it will not collapse. Cut a piece of cardboard to fit on top of the box so that it overlaps about ½" all around, except for the back. This will become the Jack-in-the-box's lid. With a piece of tape or a strip of cloth and some glue, hook one edge of the lid to the back of the box so that the tape or cloth works like a hinge.

So that the box can be easily carried and to allow freedom of the hands, glue or staple two straps to the front and back of the inside of the box. The exterior of the box should be suitably decorated. Use a real Jack-in-the-box as a guide. Eyeholes must be cut in the front of the box, so that "Jack" can walk around with his lid down.

A piece of tape or string should be attached to the lid and the front of the box so that the lid is kept in place when "Jack" pops out. Wear bright-colored clothing and appropriate clown make-up to simulate Jack.

Regular Clothes As Costumes

The following costumes can be made with clothing articles that are probably around the house. Second-hand and used clothing stores are also a good source for authentic costumes and accessories at reasonable prices.

Gangster

A dark, preferably double breasted suit, with a dark shirt and a white tie create the basics for a gangster costume. A carnation or fake flower in the lapel, a big cigar and a violin case should be added. A wide brim hat provides the final touch.

Harpo Marx

Harpo can be created with a plaid shirt, a plain pair of baggy trousers supported by a pair of suspenders and an oversized rain or trench coat.

A cheap red or yellow curly wig can be used or bits of yellow yarn can be attached to the inside of a novelty crushed top hat. All that's needed to complete the costume is Harpo's taxi horn.

Pirate

This costume requires either a full-sleeved white shirt or a tattered sleeved shirt open at the neck and tied at the waist. Wear dark pants, preferably black, which are tattered at the bottom. A head scarf can be made by using a triangular piece of cloth. A sash for the waist can be made from a piece of material 8" wide × 72" long. Another option is to mark an undershirt with a black magic marker to make a striped shirt worn underneath the outer shirt. A big gold earring, an eye patch and sword can be added as accessories.

Lady Pirate

Use a white sleeved blouse open at the neck and tied in a knot under the bust. Wear either black shorts or a short black skirt tattered at the bottom. Use a piece of cloth 8" wide × 72" long to make a sash for the waist. A red kerchief should be worn around the head. An earring and sword make the costume complete.

Wolfman

Wear an old plaid flannel shirt, and an old pair of ragged trousers, preferably corduroy. Use a piece of rope for a belt. See chapter 4 for step by step instructions for the make-up needed to complete this creature.

Period Costume

Regular clothes can be easily altered to create a "Roaring Twenties" look. For example, rolling up a pants' leg and securing it with a rubber band or a piece of elastic changes ordinary slacks into knickers, just as in the photograph of the golfer. Other accessories such as caps, vests, ties and long socks, can all be used to create a period costume.

Gypsy

Use almost any type of white or colorful blouse and wear as many strings of beads or necklaces as possible to form the basic top of the costume.

Use a colorful full skirt, and add trim if desired. Tie a long strip of colorful material around the waist for a sash and let the ends hang down at one side. Boots, a head scarf, an earring, and a piece of lace or shawl thrown over the shoulders adds the final touch.

Hobo

This is one of the easiest costumes to construct. Wear ill-fitting patched clothes—the more holes and tears the better—and a rumpled old hat. Make-up can be used to simulate an Emmett Kelly-type circus clown.

Pajama Costumes

Sleeper pajamas can be used for almost any type of animal costume. Keep in mind that sleeper pajamas are also made for adults, so that their use is not limited to children's costumes.

Most sleeper pajamas are made of a soft, fuzzy material that can be easily dyed at home. By adding the proper sets of ears to a hood, as shown in the diagram, and a tail, pajamas can be used to simulate anything from a mouse to a rabbit.

Sleeper pajamas can also be used for non-animal costumes, such as a mummy or other monsters. A few ideas are provided below.

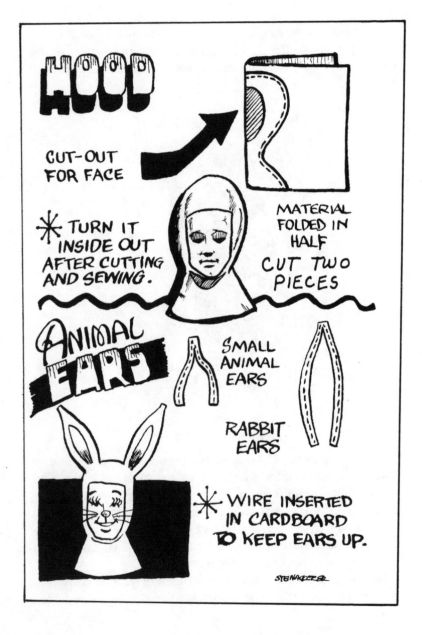

HOOD

CUT-OUT FOR FACE

* TURN IT INSIDE OUT AFTER CUTTING AND SEWING.

MATERIAL FOLDED IN HALF

CUT TWO PIECES

ANIMAL EARS

SMALL ANIMAL EARS

RABBIT EARS

* WIRE INSERTED IN CARDBOARD TO KEEP EARS UP.

STEINACKER

Rabbit

Attach a large cotton ball to the back of the pajamas to form a bunny tail. A hood and ears should be made out of the same color material as the pajamas, and a large pink or blue bow can be tied around the neck to help disguise the difference between materials.

Sew two pieces of material together to form bunny ears. Slip a piece of cardboard or light-weight wire into the ears to stiffen them. Sew, glue or pin the ears to the hood. Use make-up to create a pink nose, an eyebrow pencil to draw whiskers.

Lion

For the lion's mane, cut a piece of furry or plush material to go over the head and rest on the shoulders. Another piece of this material should be sewn to the hood to enhance the effect.

The pajamas should be dyed yellow or golden brown. The tail and ears can be created using the same principles for the Bunny Costume. The lion's face should be made with yellow face paint, and whiskers can be drawn on with an eyebrow pencil.

Mummy

Dip strips of gauze or another thin material into a pot of strong coffee to tint the material the proper color. Stretch the material out and allow it to dry before glueing or stitching it to the pajamas.

Make a hood as shown in the diagram. While the mummy is wearing the hood, someone must wrap the gauze or strips of cloth around the head so that it is completely covered. Then, either glue or stitch the cloth around the face. Cut away the material covering the eyes, nose and mouth, and apply make-up to tint the face the same color as the costume. Strips of the material should be glued to thin cotton gloves and shoes to complete the effect.

Gowns, Robes and Capes

All of the following costumes can be made with a minimum of sewing, glueing or pinning using an old academic gown or choir robe. If these items are not available, a substitute can be easily made. First, cut a tabard from a large piece of material, as shown in the diagram on page 30.

Next, make an "over-robe," as shown below, to be worn over the tabard.

Tie a cord or sash around the waist as shown in the diagram, to create the proper effect.

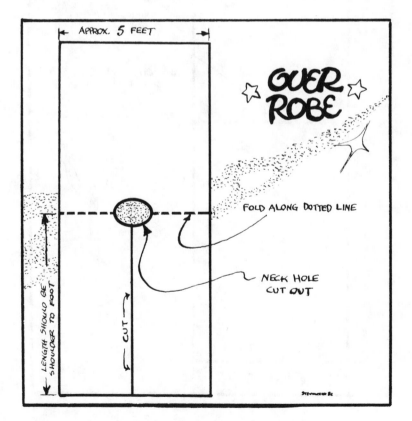

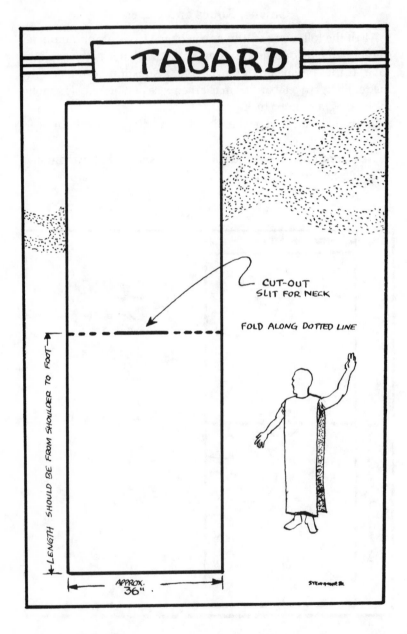

TABARD

CUT-OUT
SLIT FOR NECK

FOLD ALONG DOTTED LINE

← LENGTH SHOULD BE FROM SHOULDER TO FOOT →

APPROX.
36"

BEFORE   AFTER

Some of the costumes in this section require a cape. To make a full size cape, use a piece of wide material and cut a full circle in it (see diagram.) A small section should be cut from the center of the circle for neck space. Next, cut a straight line from the edge of the cape to the opening for the neck. Two small pieces of fabric can be pinned or sewed to the opening by the neck for tie strings.

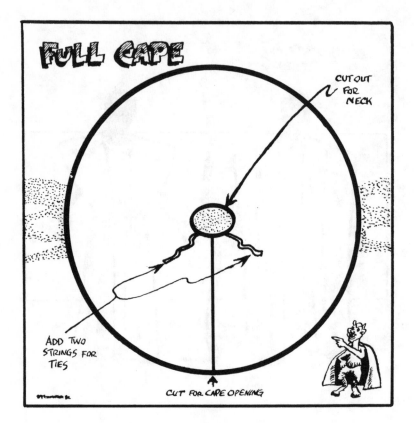

FULL CAPE

CUT OUT FOR NECK

ADD TWO STRINGS FOR TIES

CUT FOR CAPE OPENING

Ghoul

Use a black academic gown or choir robe. A black tabard is worn over this and a white cord is tied around the waist. If a gown or robe is not available, make a black tabard and cover this with a black over-robe.

Add a long flowing black cape, following the cape pattern, and drape an extra piece of black material over the head for a hood. Use appropriate ghoulish make-up as described in chapter 4.

Witch

Use a black gown or robe. If one is not available, make a black tabard and wear a black over-robe. A dark colored cord should be tied around the waist. A cape makes a nice addition, as does a broom.

For the witch's hat, cut a large circle out of a piece of cardboard corresponding to the correct head size, as shown in the diagram. Make a cardboard cone, and glue it to the circle. Cover the hat with black crepe paper. Use an extra piece of paper to form a hat band. See chapter 4 for make-up ideas.

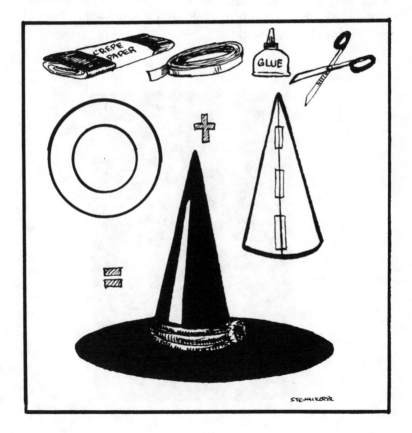

Sheik

Use a white robe or gown, or make a white tabard. An over-robe, made in a darker color such as black or burgundy, should be worn over top.

Place a 3–4 foot square piece of white material on a table and fold one corner toward the center of the square. Place the material on your head with the folded point near the center of the head. The longest part of the cloth should be hanging down toward the center of the back. Secure the cloth to the head by tying a piece of rope or a narrow strip of fabric around the cloth twice, tying it in the rear and letting the ends hang down. It is best to show a bit of the white fabric between the forehead and the rope. Finally, take the right side of the head piece under the chin and place it over the left shoulder.

Angel

Use a white robe or gown for the basic costume, or make a white tabard. A piece of gold cord or fabric should be woven around the robe or tabard. Make a long white over-robe and wear this over either the white tabard or the robe.

To form a halo, use aluminum clothes line wire to form a smaller circle—head size—within a larger one, as shown, Connect the circles with strong adhesive tape. Gold Christmas garland should be wrapped around the halo. Wings are a good addition and can be made from foam rubber or aluminum wire and wrapped with gold Christmas garland.

Comedy Costumes

These costumes are a bit more elaborate and some require a lot of effort. The results, however, are guaranteed to be rewarding.

Tax Payer

No matter whether it's called "the tax payer, a gambler's dilemma, or a getting down to the bare facts," a barrel makes a wonderful comedy costume.

The barrel may be held in place by securely attaching a pair of wide suspenders to it. Depending on the party, anything from a bathing suit to a pair of long johns can be worn.

Turkey

This can be a hilarious costume, but it does require a lot of work.

The basic body, legs and wings of the turkey are made from cardboard boxes, held together with tape, and covered with cloth. The beak and feet are cut out of cloth, while the eyes are ping pong balls with buttons attached. A piece of wire may be used to help support the neck. By attaching a pair of suspenders, as in the barrel costume, the turkey can be carried without the use of the hands.

To give the impression of riding on top of the turkey, wear tights or long underwear which will give the impression of turkey legs. Wear a dark jacket, and pin it closed at the neck. A collar and cuffs can be cut out of paper or cloth and pinned to the jacket. A pair of pants, stuffed with newspaper and pinned or tied to the body of the turkey, enhance the effect. Although the photograph depicts a turkey, the same principles could be used for almost any type of animal costume.

Freudian Slip

Cover a large book with plain paper cover and print "Sigmund Freud" on the cover. Wear a lady's slip and beard and claim to be a *Freudian Slip*.

The Whistler

This is one of the most bizarre costumes, but also one of the funniest.

Use red make-up to draw lips *around* the navel. The eyes and nose can be drawn on the stomach with make-up, and a novelty nose and ears may be glued to the body with spirit gum. A large

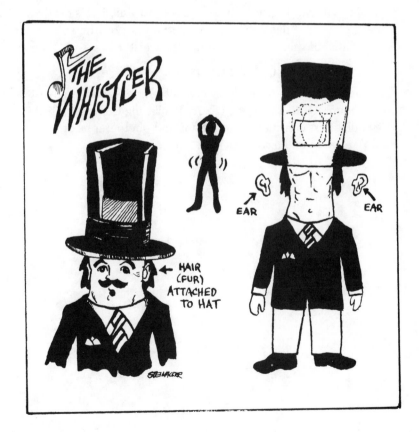

hat, made from cardboard, should be worn over the head and arms as shown in the diagram. An opening should be cut out of the hat so that vision is not impaired. The opening can be covered with a wire screening so that others can't look in.

Cover the top of the trousers with a fake shirt collar and a pre-knotted neck tie. Then button a sport coat around the waist. This should extend to the area around the knees. Stuff the arms with newspaper and add a pair of gloves to the ends of the sleeves. Moving the stomach in and out causes the navel, disguised as a pair of lips, to whistle a happy tune.

The Flasher

A rain coat, bathing suit, shoes and socks are all that is needed to be the classic "flasher." To put a little light on the subject, wear a small flashing lantern around the waist.

Creative Costumes

For additional costume ideas, consult Mark Walker's newest book, *Creative Costumes* ($4.95, Liberty Publishing Company, Inc.). The book offers complete descriptions and photographs of more than 70 easy-to-make costumes for any occasion.

MAKE-UP

Character make-up takes time to prepare and apply, but th results are well worth the effort. This chapter contains step-by-step instructions for creating several of the more traditional Halloween characters.

Before applying any make-up, there are a few simple rules that should be followed.

- If you know or suspect that you have sensitive skin, it is best to apply a little make-up to a tender area on your arm. If the skin appears to be sensitive after one hour, then you should probably not apply make-up to your face.

- It is best to use a name-brand make-up from an established company with a good reputation. A few such companies are the M. Stein Cosmetic Company, Ben Nye, Krylon and Bob Kelly. Their make-up can generally be purchased from local costume shops or mail-ordered from the list of suppliers in the back of this book.

- *DO NOT* try to substitute home-made make-up such as dyes, shoe polish, water-color paint, glues, etc., for professional make-up. Those items can be extremely dangerous.

- Be very careful when applying make-up in the areas of the eyes and mouth.

- When removing make-up, be sure not to rub it into the pores. Use a make-up remover and gently wipe the make-up from the face with a soft cloth.

- This chapter contains references to the use of liquid latex. It is extremely important that you *DO NOT* apply latex over any facial hair, as it is impossible to remove without a great deal of pain. However, liquid latex is extremely easy to remove from the face by gently pulling it off.

- To remove a false nose, chin or crepe hair that has been glued to the face with spirit gum, gently pull the piece away from the face and remove the glue with spirit gum remover. Important: spirit gum *can not* be removed with soap and water. Any attempt to do so will irritate the skin.

- If you are really serious about applying character make-up in a professional manner rather than in an amateurish way, it is highly recommended that you practice several times before Halloween night. This will cut the application time in half and you will arrive at the party on time instead of a day late.

When this chapter refers to color make-up, it will be available in many forms—stick, creme, pancake, liquid, liner, etc. If the entire face is to be covered with a particular color, it is suggested that either make-up creme, liquid or pancake be used. Use a make-up stick or a liner to shade in areas of the face for lines and shadows.

In the next few pages the models, pictured on page 42, will undergo startling transformations. Study them closely—you'll be amazed to see what a little make-up and ingenuity can do!

Clown

Materials needed:

powder puff	black eyebrow pencil
white powder	black and red make-up
baby brush or soft paint brush	false nose
clown white	wig
sponge	make-up remover

When applying clown make-up, neatness is the most important factor. Every color should have a sharp, clean edge with no smearing.

Step 1. Using a black eyebrow pencil, outline the desired features for the eyebrows, lips, etc.

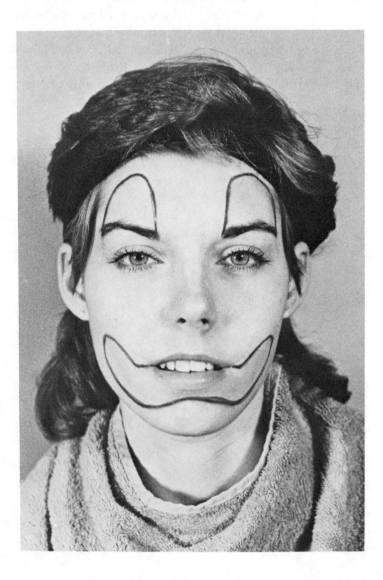

Step 2. Using fingers or a sponge, apply an even coat of clown white to the areas of the face that will not be colored in red or black. Come as close to the outline as possible without touching it.

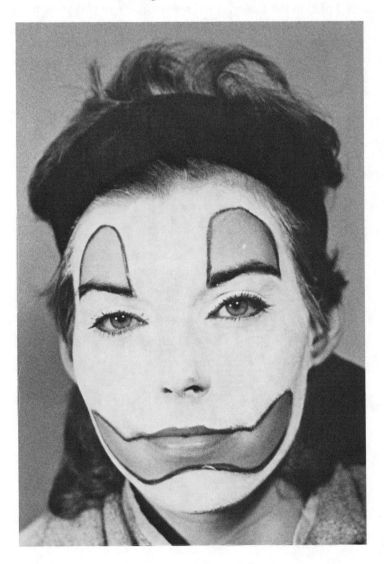

Step 3. Fill in the eyebrows with black make-up. Trace around the outer edge with the black eyebrow pencil, filling in between the black and white and leaving a neat clean line.

Step 4. Fill in the lips with red make-up, coming as close to the inside of the outline as possible. Using the black eyebrow pencil, fill in between the white on the face and the red on the lips, making certain the lines are sharp and clean.

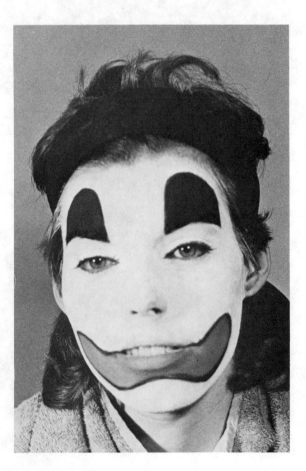

Step 5. If grease paint is used, the entire face *must* be powdered. Use a soft brush to remove the excess powder.

Step 6. A false nose may be purchased from a costume shop or made from nose putty or a round ball. Attach the false nose with spirit gum or a piece of thin white elastic.

Step 7. Add a brightly colored novelty wig. Either buy one or take an old wig, brush it out, and spray it with bright-colored hair spray.

Ghoul

Materials needed:
clown white
bald pate
liquid latex
brown and black eyebrow
   pencil
brown, black and yellow
   make-up

translucent powder
powder puff
baby brush or soft paint brush
make-up remover

Ghoulish make-up can be used with many Halloween costumes, from the Grim Reaper to Charon, the ferryman of the
River Styx.

Step 1. Place the bald pate on the head as illustrated.

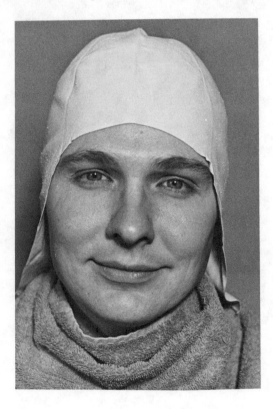

Step 2. Seal the edges of the bald pate to the face with liquid latex, applying as many coats as necessary to fill in the ridge between the face and the pate.

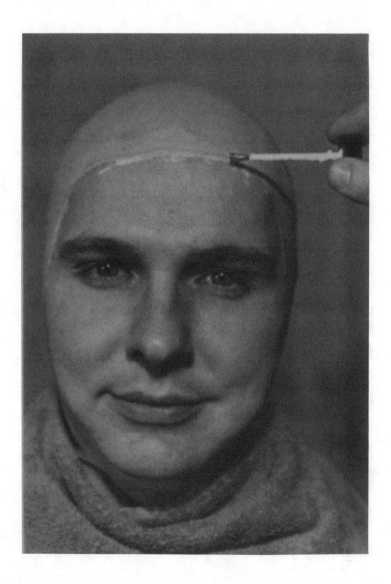

Step 3. Outline the areas shown in the photograph with a black
        eyebrow pencil.

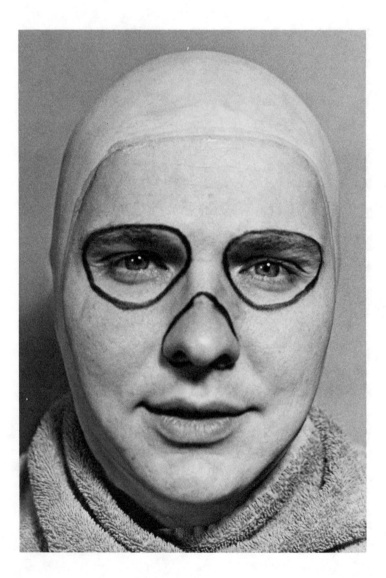

Step 4. Apply a coat of clown white over the entire face and *head*, excluding the penciled-in areas.

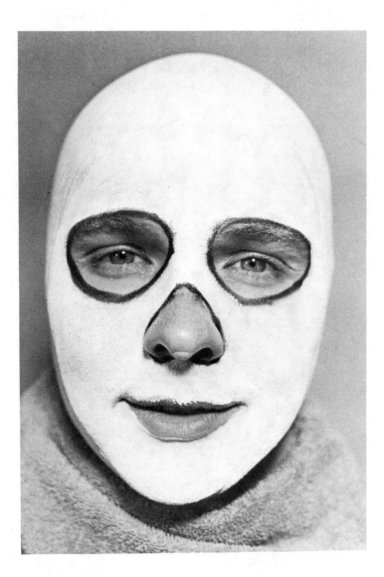

Step 5. Fill in the outlined areas with black and brown make-up as shown.

Step 6. Draw in the skull and lip lines, using black and brown eyebrow pencils.

Step 7. Blend some of the brown and yellow colors into the clown white covering the face and head to create a bone-like color.

Step 8. Powder the entire face and head with translucent powder and remove the excess with a soft brush.

Ghoulish make-up will work best when a black, hooded robe is worn. See the costume chapter for instructions.

Old Age

Materials needed:
liquid latex
sponge
powder puff
translucent powder
baby brush or soft paint brush
brown or maroon eyebrow
   pencil

brown, grey or dark maroon
   make-up
silver/grey hair spray or liquid
   hair whitener
make-up remover
hair dryer

Wrinkles, shadows and grey hair help create the illusion of old age.

Step 1. Using a brown or maroon eyebrow pencil, draw lines to form the wrinkles as shown in the photograph. Look in the mirror, wrinkle your forehead and face, and trace the natural lines.

Step 2. Use a make-up that is darker than your skin color (such as brown, grey or dark maroon) to shadow in the areas as shown in the photograph. With the fingers, blend the lines so that there are no sharp edges.

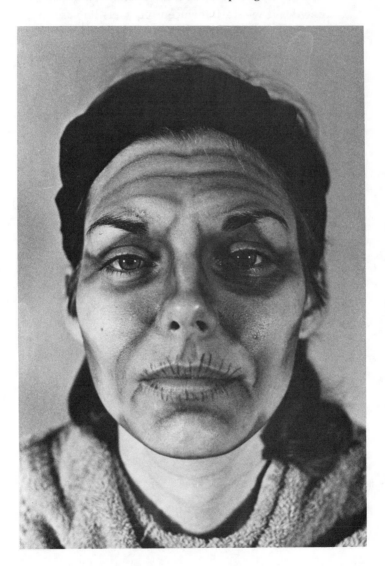

Step 3. Using two hands, stretch the skin as much as possible in the area outside the corner of the eye. Have a friend apply a thick coat of liquid latex on that area. Using a hair dryer, dry the latex until it is transparent and then powder it with a translucent powder. Be sure to keep the skin very taut until the powder has been applied.

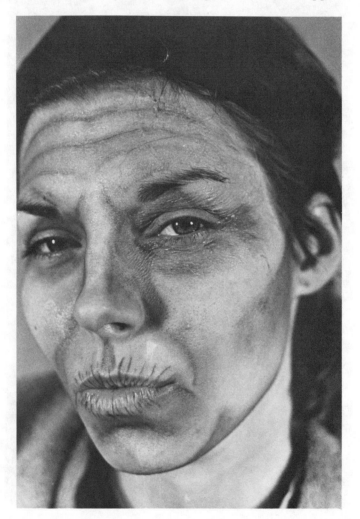

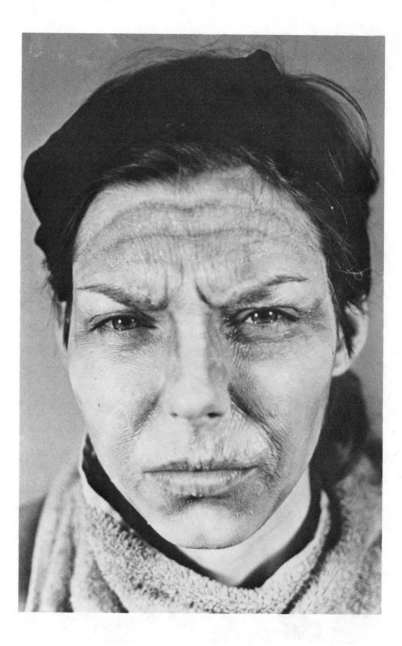

Step 4. Move on to different sections of the face and repeat the process until the entire face is covered. When this is completed, brush off the excess powder. *NOTE:* Be sure not to apply the liquid latex over any facial hair, such as eyebrows, beards or moustaches.

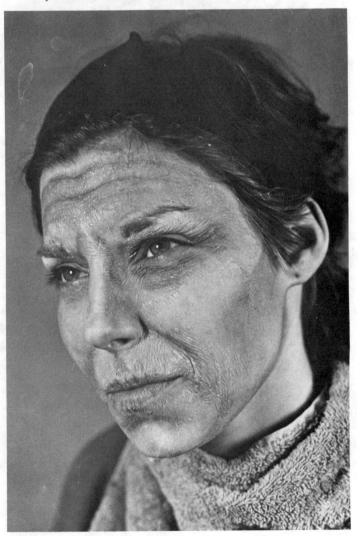

Step 5. If possible, obtain a grey wig. If one is not available, style the hair like an older person would and color it with silver/grey hair spray or liquid hair whitener. Make certain the eyebrows are also colored white or grey.

Step 6. For a final touch, wear an old-style pair of glasses.

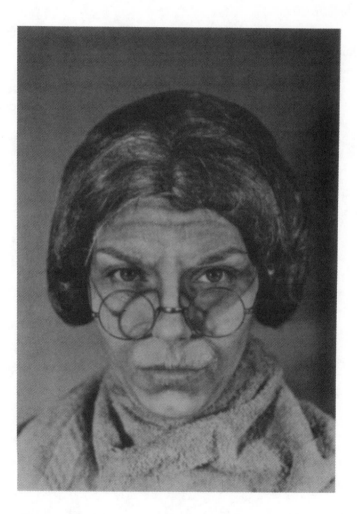

Vampire

Materials needed:

clown white	fangs
grey, black and red make-up	white powder
black eyebrow pencil	powder puff
sponge	baby brush or soft paint brush
black-colored hair spray	make-up remover
hair spray	

Different accents of color over a white base can create the illusion of the living dead.

Step 1. If the traditional Dracula appearance is desired, the hair should be washed, combed straight back, and allowed to dry tight to the head. A touch of hair spray will hold the hair into position. If you do not have dark or black hair, it can be easily tinted with black-colored hair spray.

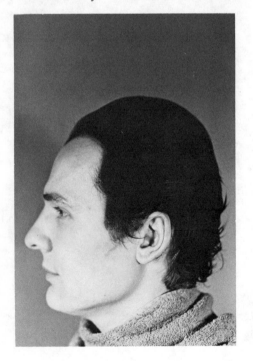

Step 2. Use a black eyebrow pencil to sketch a widow's peak on the forehead, and to shape the eyebrows as shown.

Step 3 Apply a very thin coat of clown white over the entire
face, excluding the penciled in areas.

Step 4 Apply either black or grey make-up with the fingers or a
sponge to shade in the areas around the eyes, nose and
cheeks as illustrated.

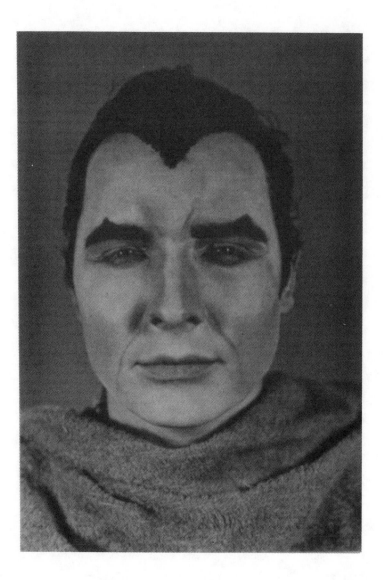

Step 5 *Thin* red lips tend to give the vampire an evil appearance.
Powder the entire face with white powder and remove
the excess with a soft brush. For the right bite, add fangs.

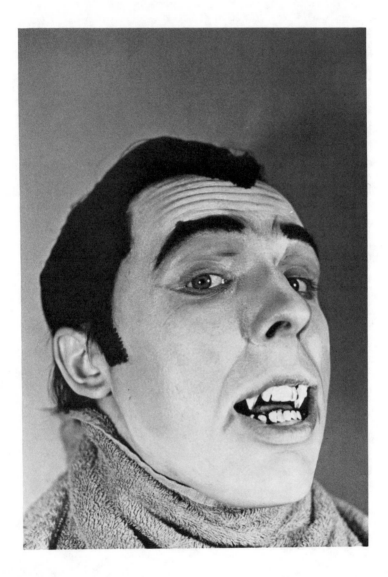

Witch

Materials needed:

false nose	baby brush or soft paint brush
false chin	translucent powder
nose putty	powder puff
spirit gum	black tooth wax
sponge	wig
green make-up	make-up remover
brown, black and grey make-up	spirit gum remover
clown white	

The most recognizable features of a witch are a long pointed nose, a sharp chin, long straggly hair, and an overall evil appearance.

Step 1. A long witch nose and pointed chin can be bought at a costume shop or novelty store. Apply a thin coat of spirit gum to the inside edge of the nose and chin where they will make contact with the face. Allow the spirit gum to become tacky before placing the false nose and chin in place.

The nose and chin can also be made out of nose putty. Soften a small amount of nose putty and apply it to the nose and chin. If your skin is oily or if you tend to perspire, apply a thin coat of spirit gum before applying the nose putty. Shape the putty to form the desired features, and add a bump or wart to the nose or chin. To seal the nose putty, apply two coats of spirit gum over it. Be sure to allow the first coat to dry before applying the second.

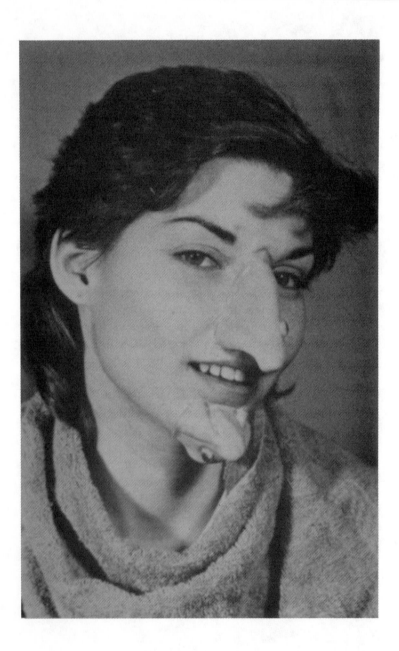

Step 2. Use a sponge to apply an even coat of green make-up to the *entire* face, being careful not to damage the sculptured nose and chin.

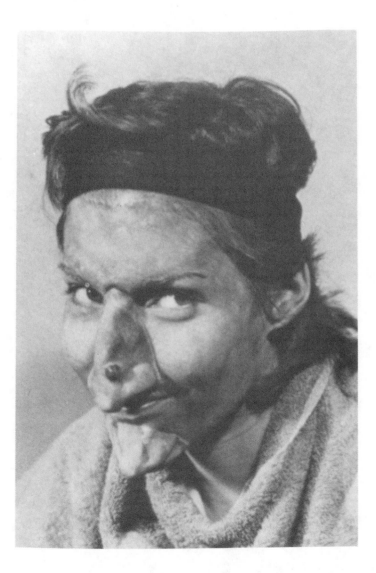

Step 3. Use a darker tone make-up, such as black, brown or grey to shadow in the areas as illustrated in the photograph.

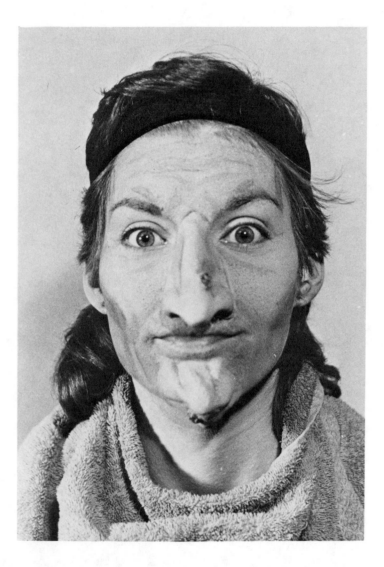

Step 4. Use white make-up or clown white to apply highlights. Blend the white into the green base make-up, as shown in the photograph, with the fingers or a sponge.

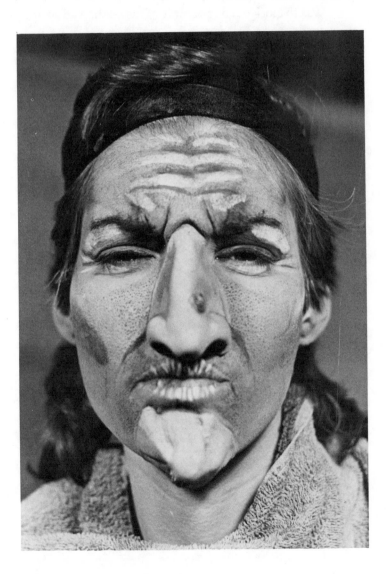

Step 5. Apply a translucent powder over the entire face. Allow it to set for a few minutes before brushing off the excess powder.

Step 6. For finishing touches, apply a small dab of black tooth wax to block out one or more of the teeth. Add a straggly wig.

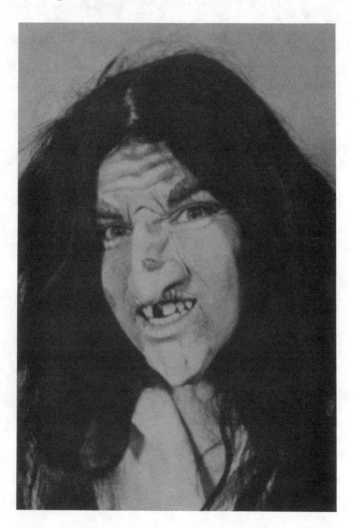

Wolfman

Materials needed:

fangs	crepe hair
black and brown make-up	spirit gum
nose putty	spirit gum remover
werewolf nose	make-up remover
werewolf ears (optional)	

A Wolfman character is always effective, especially if there is a full moon on Halloween night.

Step 1. Apply a thin coat of spirit gum to the inside edge of a rubber werewolf nose where it will make contact with the face. Allow the spirit gum to become tacky before attaching the false nose.

The nose can also be made out of nose putty. Soften a small amount of nose putty and apply it to the nose. If your skin is oily or if you tend to perspire, apply a thin coat of spirit gum before applying the nose putty. Shape the putty as shown in the photograph. Apply two coats of spirit gum over the putty to seal it. Be sure to allow the first coat to dry before applying the second.

Step 2. Apply the brown make-up to the areas of the face as
shown.

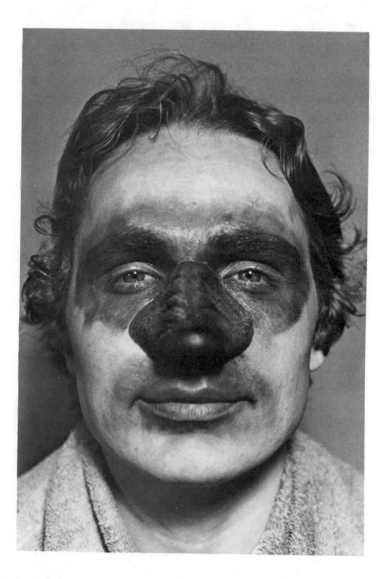

Step 3. Crepe hair, in its original state, is braided. There is a
string holding the braid together. Cut this string and
unravel the braid; the hair will be curly. To remove the
curls, separate the hair as shown in the photograph and
straighten by pressing with a steam iron. Pull off sections about 2–3 inches long and apply to the face as
described in the following steps.

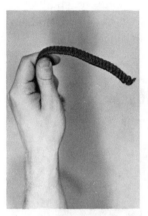 

 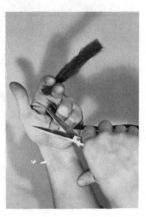

Step 4. Use an eyebrow pencil to divide the forehead into 3 equal horizontal sections. At line #1, apply a thin coat of spirit gum across the forehead, about 1-inch wide. Apply 3 inch long pieces of crepe hair so that it hangs vertically. Glue only the lower part of this layer of hair. Move the upper part of this layer away from the face and apply spirit gum along line #2. Once again, apply 3 inch-long pieces of crepe hair along line #2, and repeat this procedure with line #3. Gently brush all the crepe hair upwards so that it blends together, and the top layers blend into the real hair.

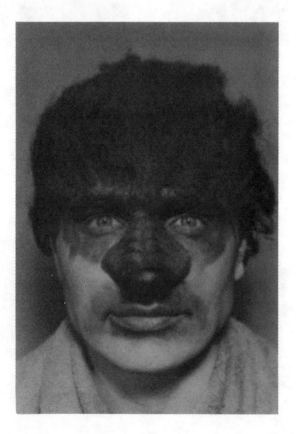

Step 5. Starting under the eyes, follow the same procedure in step #4. Apply the spirit gum and crepe hair so that the hair hangs down and covers the entire face and neck.

Step 6. Blend black make-up into the brown areas around the eyes, ears and mouth to achieve a leathery effect.

Step 7. Use a sharp knife to change a plastic set of fangs into realistic werewolf teeth by scratching and cutting some of the portions away from the shiny white teeth. Rub a little brown and black make-up into the crevices.

Step 8. Apply crepe hair and make-up to the hands and color the fingernails black for a more realistic werewolf. Rubber werewolf ears are optional.

CHILDRENS'
HALLOWEEN PARTIES

In recent years, many church groups and community organizations (not to mention parents) have begun to sponsor Halloween parties and activities as an alternative to trick-or-treating and to provide a night of safe games and fun for their children. If your group is planning a children's Halloween party or if your child has talked you into giving one for his friends, this chapter is for you! It includes ideas for invitations, games, fortune-telling, magic tricks and refreshments. (See Chapter 7 for Halloween decoration ideas.)

The suggestions in this chapter are designed for children between the ages of 5 and 11. In general, most children under four are really too young for Halloween fun—they're too easily frightened. Likewise, most children of twelve and up are ready for the activities described in Chapter 6, "Adult Halloween Parties." You'll be able to pick and choose from the activities in this chapter to fit the age group that you'll be entertaining.

Let your child or the children in your group help you plan the party. This provides children with a sense of responsibility and accomplishment, and allows them to exercise their fertile imaginations. You'll probably find some of their ideas to be useful—and maybe better than yours!

Planning, of course, is the key to a successful party, especially where children are involved. Here is a check list for this purpose.

2 WEEKS BEFORE: ● Decide on date and time;
                 ● Make guest list and send invitations;
                 ● Select games and make prop list;
                 ● Plan the menu;
                 ● Select prizes;
                 ● Select decorations.

3 DAYS BEFORE: ● Gather materials and props for decora-
                   tions, games, prizes, and other activities;
                 ● Check invitation responses and make final
                   guest list;
                 ● Prepare gifts and prize bags;
                 ● Plan party schedule.

PARTY DAY   ● Decorate the party room or hall;
(MORNING)   ● Organize all game and activity props in
                   a convenient area;
                 ● Prepare foods;
                 ● Display prizes and gifts.

(WHEN GUESTS   ● Greet all guests at door;
ARRIVE)   ● Begin a "warm-up" game for early arriv-
                   als;
                 ● Follow pre-planned party schedule.

For the sake of clarity, the following pages are written as if your child is going to host the party in his home, but remember that these ideas can be applied to larger parties for church groups and other organizations. In any case, this chapter contains the ingredients for a "frighteningly" successful Halloween party. The rest is up to you!

Invitations

Commercial party invitations are available at any card shop or gift store. But why not help your child design and make his own? All that's needed is construction paper, a black felt tip pen and/ or a white marking pen, a piece of cardboard, and scissors.

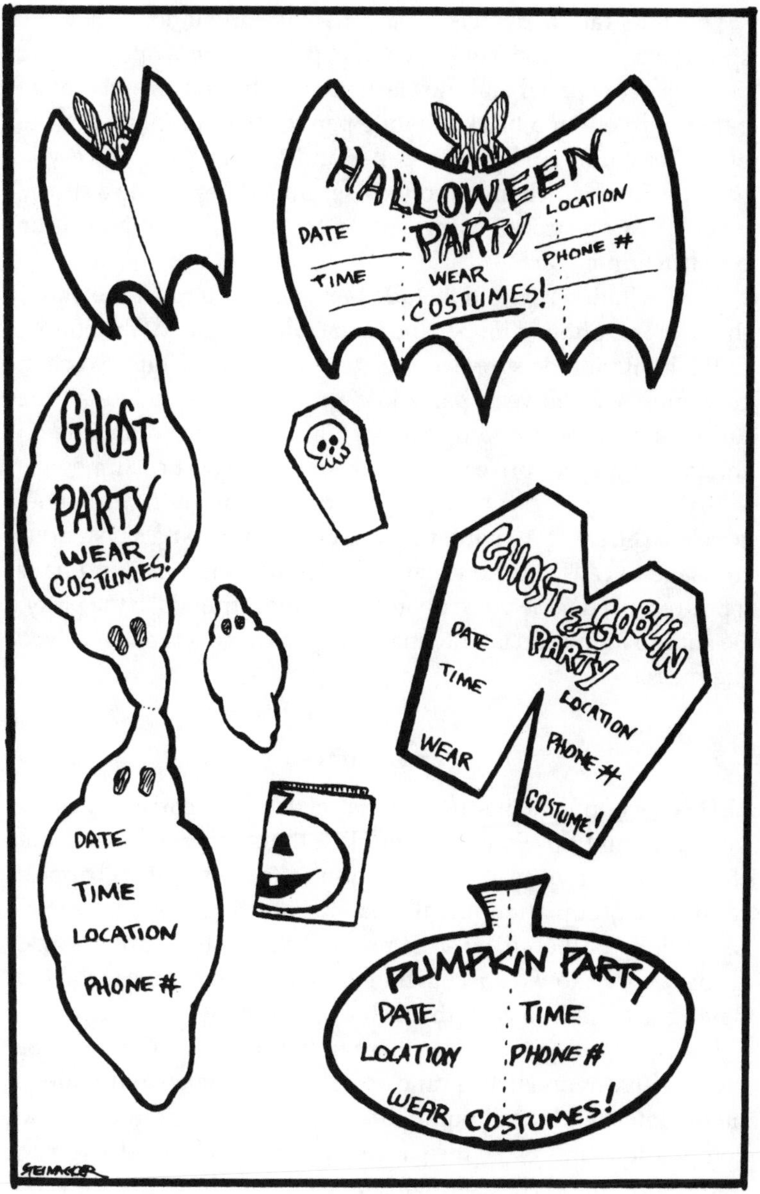
HALLOWEEN
PARTY
DATE
TIME
LOCATION
PHONE #
WEAR
COSTUMES!
GHOST
PARTY
WEAR
COSTUMES!
DATE
TIME
LOCATION
PHONE #
GHOST & GOBLIN
PARTY
DATE
TIME
WEAR
LOCATION
PHONE #
COSTUME!
PUMPKIN PARTY
DATE
TIME
LOCATION
PHONE #
WEAR COSTUMES!
STEINMACHER

The illustration depicts 4 easy-to-make invitations. For the spooky bat, use black construction paper and the white marking pen. Use grey paper and the black pen for the coffin, and orange paper with either a black or white pen for the pumpkin. For the ghost, of course, use white paper and a black pen. Once you have decided which invitation to use, cut its shape from a sturdy piece of cardboard allowing you to trace the invitation on the construction paper.

The invitations should include the date and time of the party, the address, phone number and your child's name. At the bottom of the invitation be sure to stipulate that everyone must come in costume. A Halloween party just isn't the same unless all the guests are dressed appropriately. You may want to include on the invitation that prizes will be given for the best costumes.

If you have or can borrow a telephone answering machine, here's a different invitation idea. Mail each guest a mysterious message to call your house at a certain day and time, and have a pre-recorded eerie voice invite your child's friends to the party. Be sure to follow-up later to make certain that everyone received the message.

Party Games

This section contains 10 different Halloween party games for younger children. Some are simple, others more elaborate, but they are all fun to play. Be sure to select games that will appeal to the age group attending the party. Fourth graders, for example, might be bored by a game kindergarten children would enjoy. Also, allow a specific time period for the games to avoid having the children rush through the rest of the party activities.

It's a good idea to award prizes to the winners. These can be inexpensive items such as candy bars, rubber snakes and spiders, model kites, and small pumpkins. Prizes will spark interest and competition, and make the games more entertaining. However, make sure that *every* child wins at least one prize, even if it's a booby prize for last place.

Apples on a String

This traditional Halloween game is still an old favorite. It is also a great way of keeping the early arrivals busy when the party is just starting.

Tie a piece of string to several large apples, and suspend each from a pipe or door frame to the approximate height of the children. With their hands behind their backs, each child tries to take bites out of the apples as they swing back and forth.

A prize can be awarded to the child who eats the most of his or her apple.

Pumpkin Says

Younger children will love this game. All it requires is several toy balloons (preferably orange), and paper and pencil.

Cut the paper into as many 5" by 1" strips as there are balloons. On each strip, print a different Halloween-related stunt that each child can perform, such as:

- Walk like Frankenstein
- Creep like a cat
- Hoot like an owl
- Grin like a jack-o'-lantern
- Walk like a wobbly skeleton
- Flap your arms like a bat
- Make a sound like a creaking door

Roll up the strips, and insert one in each balloon. Inflate the balloons, and tie a short piece of string to the end of each one. Hang the balloons from the ceiling, either scattered throughout the room or clustered together in a corner. When the time comes to play the game, each child picks a balloon. An adult will then pop the balloon, remove the paper, and read it aloud. Each child then does what "Pumpkin Says." This game will probably work best if each child has at least 2 stunts to perform.

Peanut Pumpkin Toss

Carve out a pumpkin, and instead of cutting out a nose, eyes, and a mouth to make a jack-o'-lantern, draw these on the pumpkin with a black magic marker.

Place the pumpkin on the floor at the end of the room and use masking tape to put a line on the floor about 10 feet away from it. Give each child 15 peanuts, and have each take a turn trying to toss 5 peanuts, one at a time, into the pumpkin. After each child's turn, the pumpkin should be emptied, and a running score kept.

After each child has had three turns, tally the score and announce the winner. A good prize for this game could be all of the peanuts that were used.

Who Am I

Have everyone sit on the floor in a circle. Blindfold one of the children, spin him around a few times, and help him take a seat inside the circle.

The blindfolded child now touches one person at a time and asks, "Who are you?" The child responds using a disguised voice, saying something that relates to Halloween. For example, "I am a

- Cat
- Pumpkin
- Witch
- Skeleton
- Ghost

Before the game begins, give some sample responses, and let the children know that it's not necessary to use a different word each time.

The blindfolded child tries to decide who has answered him, going around the circle until he guesses right. He then changes places with the other child and the game continues.

Num-Skull

This game is the Halloween version of "Hot Potato." Instead of a potato, use a small plastic skull, which can be purchased at any novelty store or magic shop.

Once again, the children should be sitting in a circle on the floor. Hand the skull to the nearest child, and tell the group to toss it to one another until they hear you blow a whistle or sound a horn, etc. The child holding the skull when the whistle blows is out, and the remaining players move closer together to form a tighter circle.

The game continues until only one child—the winner—is left. An ideal prize for this game would be the skull itself.

Comedy Mindreading

Here is a funny game for older children. Two friends should practice the routine so that it can be performed smoothly, using some of the ideas below.

During the party, someone declares that his friend can read minds, and that they can prove it. He claims that his friend will be able to identify any object or read anyone's mind by the "psychic energy" generated between the two of them. The mindreader is blindfolded, and stands at the end of the room with his back towards the other guests. His accomplice begins to walk around the room, saying "As I touch any object or as I think of one, the mindreader will tell you what is it!"

He walks over and touches someone's shoe. "What am I touching?" The mindreader does not know. "Come on, *step* on it," he says. "A shoe!" shouts the mindreader. "Correct! Amazing!" says the accomplice.

Next he picks up a pencil. "What am I holding in my hand?" he says. Again, the mindreader does not know. "Get to the point! Come on, get the *lead* out," says the accomplice. "A pencil!" the mindreader says. "Right again!"

"What color is Mary's blue costume, oh great mindreader?" The mindreader pauses, concentrating. "Red, green, no, blue!" "Correct, oh great one!"

Next, he picks up a handkerchief. "What am I holding in my hand?" The mindreader does not know. "Come on, don't blow it, this is nothing to *sneeze* about." "A handkerchief!" "Right again!"

The accomplice then asks someone to pick a number between 1 and 10. "Without saying what the number is, hold up the number of fingers which represents it," he says. The person (for example) holds up three fingers. "Oh great mindreader," says the accomplice, "I'm thinking of a number between two and four!" Again, the mindreader concentrates, and then exclaims "6, 9, no, wait, 3!" "Right once more!"

The possibilities for this mindreading "demonstration" are limitless. With a little bit of extra practice, the pair may easily come up with clues which are not at all obvious to the participants, yet perfectly clear to each other.

Ghost Stories

A ghost story session is a must for a children's Halloween party, so long as the stories aren't *too* scary. Remember, children are impressionable, so use good judgment. The local librarian will be able to suggest appropriate stories for the age group attending the party.

The right atmosphere for spooky stories can be created by dimming the lights and placing a grinning jack-o'-lantern, equipped with a burning candle, in the middle of the room. A green spotlight could also cast an eerie glow. The adult reading the stories should be sitting either next to the pumpkin, or under the green light in order to have enough light to read by. All the children should sit on the floor close to the reader. It's a good idea for the reader to be familiar with the stories so that the right words can be accented, the proper sound effects inserted, and a suspenseful mood sustained throughout.

An alternative to reading ghost stories is to have the children use their imaginations to create their own spooky tales. Tell them that you will start a story, and that each of them will take a turn continuing it. Here are a few "Starters":

> There was an old dark house at the end of a dimly lit street. As we opened the door, it creaked. Slowly, we crept up the stairs inside the gloomy house.

It was a cold, crisp, Halloween night. There was a full moon and a bat swooped by us as we walked out into the pumpkin patch.

It was a eerie night. There was a storm outside with thunder and several flashes of lightning. All of a sudden, the lights went out.

There was a knock on the door in the middle of the night. I crept downstairs and opened the door slowly. There stood—

No one knew what was in the old trunk, but we had to open it. As we lifted the old, heavy lid we saw—

Skeleton Paper Tear

As the ghost stories are being read or told, another adult could create a string of paper skeletons. All that's required is a sheet of newspaper, scissors and a black marking pen. Fold the paper as shown in the illustration, and trace the skeleton with the pen. Cut off the excess paper and—Presto—you've created a string of dancing skeletons!

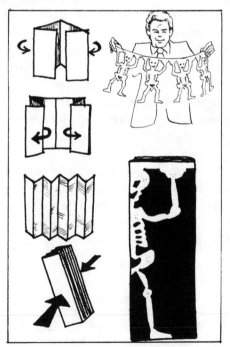

Halloween Hunt

This is the Halloween version of the Easter Egg Hunt. It can be played indoors if the party is being held in a large basement or club room, or in a recreation hall. Ideally, though, the hunt should be held outside if the weather is suitable.

Instead of eggs, the children will be hunting Halloween-related objects such as gourds, rubber spiders, plastic bats, small pumpkins, etc. These will have been previously hidden in some obvious and some not-so-easy-to-find places. Give each child a small bag, and set a time limit (15 minutes or so) for the hunt. The winner, of course, is the child who finds the most objects. Make sure that everyone finds at least one.

The Invisible Room

This game is ideal for a party held in a very large room or recreation hall. The player is taken for a tour of an "obstacle course" that has been set up, with a guide pointing out the obstacles to remember and avoid.

"Here is a small ladder," the guide says, "so step high over it . . . now we have to go around this chair . . . uh, oh, duck under that table . . . don't step in that bucket, etc."

The player is then blindfolded, and told to go through the course on his own. He steps over the ladder, walks around the chair, ducks under the table, avoids the bucket—all successfully! But why is everyone laughing? Because there are no obstacles, they've all been removed! (Quietly, after he was blindfolded.)

Four or five players can run this phantom course, so long as they are kept in another room and brought out one by one. When the blindfolds are removed, and the players realize they've been tricked, each should be rewarded with a prize for being a good sport.

Fortune Telling

A fortune telling session is the perfect opportunity for Mom or big sister to dress up as a sorceress and play the part of

"Madame Olga." This section contains several suggestions for a mysterious look into the future.

Madame Olga entices a child to sit in the chair, and to extend the palm of his hand. "Would you like your palm read?" "Yes," responds the child. She then takes a red magic marker and draws a small x on his outstretched palm. Corny, yes, but children will think it's funny.

Another child sits at the table and the sorceress inspects his palm, chanting a weird incantation and waving her hand over his. She tells him things that relate to children of his own age. For example:

A boy (or girl) in your classroom likes you.
You will do well in school this year.
You will be a successful person when you grow up.
You will live a very long life.
You will meet a special person in the near future.

She should try to inject some humor into the fortunes, and be careful *not* to embarrass the child.

Another fortune telling stunt requires a special piece of paper that is given to each child. A day or so before the party, take sheets of white paper and using milk or lemon juice and a small brush, paint a mysterious message on the paper using the liquid. When the milk or lemon juice has dried, it will become invisible. Each child who comes up to see the fortune teller must bring one of these papers. To make the fortune visible, hold it over a hot electric light bulb, and the message will turn brown and appear.

Another fortune-telling method is to give each child a sealed envelope that contains a question on a piece of paper. Each child writes his initials on the envelope, gives it to "Madame Olga," and takes a seat around the table. Madame Olga calls out the initials on each envelope as she selects it, and asks the child to stand. She then opens the envelope, and in a spooky voice, reads the question and gives the answer. Of course, the questions are known to the sorcerer, and she has her own funny answers to each one. Some examples:

Where did I leave my ring? Around the bath tub.
How many children will I have? 3—one of each.
Will I ever have my own candy store? You should, you've spend
enough money in them.
Will I ever look like a million dollars? Yes, you'll be all green and
wrinkly.

Since Madame Olga knows her guests, she can make up an
appropriate comedy future for each child.

Spooky Magic

This section contains five magic stunts simple enough to be performed by a child; ideally, the child hosting the party. The tricks require little preparation or practice, and are guaranteed to amaze and mystify.

A Present For You

The magician offers to give one of the children a present, but they first have to promise to keep the gift always. The guest opens the small box, which is packed with cotton. He pushes the cotton aside and finds—a mummy's finger—which begins to move ever so slightly!

The finger, of course, belongs to the magician. It has been powdered white, and stuck through a hole in the bottom of a small box. A bit of mercurochrome at the base of the knuckle is a nice touch.

The Magnetic Ruler

The magician announces that he has discovered a ruler that is magnetic to the human body. He rubs the ruler on his sleeve to "magnetize" it, holds it in his left hand, and slowly lifts his hand into the air. When he straightens his fingers, the ruler remains attached!

The secret, as the illustration shows, is that the magician grabs his left wrist with his right hand, extending his right forefinger against the ruler as he does so. As he uncurls the fingers of his left hand, his right finger holds the "magnetic ruler" against his hand.

Crayon Magic

The magician now claims that he can tell the color of any crayon by simply feeling it. He puts his hands behind his back, and one of the children chooses a crayon from a box of assorted colors and puts it in the magician's hands. The magician holds the crayon for a moment, concentrates, and gives it back. He then raises his left hand to his forehead, closes his eyes, and chants a magic formula. After a few seconds he reveals the correct color of the crayon!

This mystifying trick is easily done. As the magician is handed the crayon behind his back, he scrapes a small piece of it off with

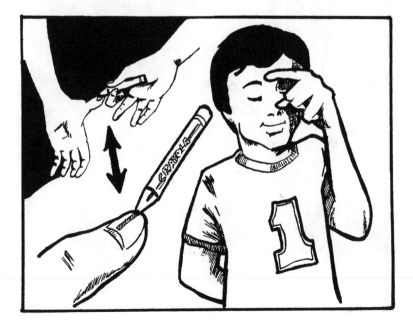

his thumbnail. As he raises his hand to his forehead, he sneaks a peek at the crayon particle on his nail, and announces the correct color.

Thirsty Spirits

The magician's next trick is to command an unseen spirit to drink a glass of water. The glass is filled and taped to a table as shown. The lights are turned off for a minute or so, during which time the magician utters a few eerie words, and then is silent. When the lights go back on, the water is gone!

All the magician needs for this trick is a straw. After the lights are turned out and he chants his magic spell, the magician quickly takes the hidden straw from his pocket, locates the glass and

quietly drinks the water. He then replaces the straw, waits a few moments, and orders the lights turned on.

Levitation

"For my last trick," says the Magician, "I will make one of you rise into the air!" He asks for two "volunteers," and asks them

to carry over a sheet-covered bench which has been sitting off to the side. One helper goes behind the bench, and the Magician and his other helper hold up one end of the sheet. The first helper lies down on the bench, and the sheet is lowered over him. Only his head and shoes are uncovered. At the Magician's command, the helper on the bench will *rise* mysteriously into the air.

In this trick, the Magician's two "volunteers" are really secret helpers, and on the bench under the sheet are two shoes attached to two long sticks. As the sheet is lifted, the secret helper to be levitated lies on the bench, but puts his feet flat on the floor. He holds the sticks under his shoulders, so that the shoes stick out from the blanket. When he is given the command to rise, he simply stands up, holding the sticks as shown in the illustration.

The children are sure to get a "rise" out of this effect.

Refreshments

Sometime during the party, the ghosts and goblins in attendance are going to get hungry, and we've included some ideas for the party menu.

The traditional candy corn kernels, apple cider, and doughnuts are always a big hit. Cookies could be shaped to form bats, faces, spiders, and snakes. Fortune cookies are also a good addition to the traditional Halloween snacks.

Spooky names can also be given to ordinary party fare, as in the sample menu below:

GOBLIN PARTY MENU
I SCREAM
GHOULASH
ZOMBIE ZODAS
SAND-WITCHES
HALLO WEENIES

The recipes listed here offer some new ideas as well as some variations on the traditional Halloween party treats.

Pumpkin Punch

INGREDIENTS
1 quart club soda
2 32-ounce cans Pineapple juice
2 quarts 7-up
2 pints orange sherbet

Mix all ingredients in a large punch bowl, except the orange sherbet. At serving time, float orange sherbet scoops on top of the punch. Serves 12.

Serve the punch from a witch's black cauldron. If you can't find a container that resembles one, make one out of papier mache and set the punch bowl inside. Better yet, hollow-out a large pumpkin and place the punch bowl inside of it.

Ghoulash

This is really a nutritious barbecue recipe, but the children will never know the difference.

INGREDIENTS
1 cup butter
1 cup chopped onions
1 cup chopped green peppers
4 8-ounce cans tomato sauce
½ cup cider vinegar
2 tablespoons liquid smoke
4 tablespoons worcestershire sauce
½ cup brown sugar
2 teaspoons dry mustard
1 teaspoon garlic powder
1 teaspoon celery seed
2 teaspoons chili powder
3 pounds ground beef
12 hamburger rolls

Melt the butter in a saucepan, add onions and peppers, and saute for 5 minutes. Add all other ingredients except ground beef, and cook for 15 minutes over low heat. Brown the ground beef in another pan and drain. Add beef to sauce and cook for 10 minutes. Serve on rolls. Serves 12.

Candied Apples

INGREDIENTS
  3   cups sugar
  1   cup light corn syrup
  1½ cups water
  1½ teaspoons red food coloring
  12 popsicle sticks
  12 medium apples

Combine sugar, syrup, water and food coloring in a large saucepan. Cook over medium heat until the mixture becomes brittle (8–10 minutes). Turn heat to low. Stick a popsicle stick into each apple (at the stem), and dip each apple into the saucepan. Place apples on waxed paper to cool and harden.

Carmel Candied Apples

INGREDIENTS
  5   tablespoons butter
  3   cups packed light brown sugar
  12 tablespoons water
  12 popsicle sticks
  12 medium apples
  clip-on candy thermometer

Combine sugar and water in a large saucepan. Mix with wooden spoon to dissolve sugar, then add butter. Cook mixture over medium heat, and bring to a boil. Cover with lid for 3 minutes, then uncover pan and turn off heat.

Clip candy thermometer to the side of the saucepan. Bring syrup to a boil over medium heat for 4 to 5 minutes, or until thermometer reads about 260°F (130°C). Turn off heat, stick a popsicle stick into each apple, dip in the mixture, and place on waxed paper to cool and harden.

Popcorn Balls

INGREDIENTS
  1½ cups sugar
  ⅔ cup apple cider
  ⅔ cup maple syrup
  ½ cup butter
  1½ teaspoons salt
  ½ teaspoon vanilla
  4 cups warm popped corn
  1 cup salted peanuts
clip-on candy thermometer

Combine sugar, cider, syrup, butter and salt in a large sauce-pan. Bring to a boil over low heat, stirring occasionally. Turn off heat, and remove crystalized sugar from sides of pan with a wet brush. Bring mixture to a boil over medium heat for 4 to 5 minutes, or until thermometer reads 260°F (130°C). Turn to low heat, and add vanilla. Turn off heat. When mixture is sufficiently cool, pour over popcorn and peanuts. Mix well, and roll into 3-inch balls. Makes 18.

Halloween Jokes And Riddles

To end the party on a happy note, treat the children to a Halloween comedy routine. Listed below are 15 Halloween-related jokes to get you started. We're sure you can think of more.

Q. What did the bird say on Halloween?
  A. TWICK OR TWEET.

Q. What color are ghosts?
  A. BOO (BLUE)

Q. What color are baby ghosts?
  A. BABY BOO (BABY BLUE)

Q. What kind of mistake does a ghost make?
  A. A BOO-BOO

Q. Why do ghosts walk at midnight?

A. BECAUSE THEY MISSED THE LAST BUS HOME.

Q. How does a witch tell time?
A. WITH HER WITCH WATCH.

Q. What time is it when a witch chases 12 trick-or-treaters down the street?
A. ONE AFTER TWELVE

Q. What is a witch's favorite subject in school?
A. SPELLING.

Q. Why couldn't the mummy come outside?
A. BECAUSE HE WAS ALL WRAPPED UP.

Q. What do you call a stupid mummy?
A. A DUMMY MUMMY

Q. What do you say to a two-headed monster?
A. HELLO, HELLO!

Q. What is the best way to communicate with a monster?
A. BY LONG DISTANCE.

Q. Where does Dracula keep his money?
A. IN A BLOOD BANK.

Q. Why isn't Dracula popular?
A. BECAUSE HE IS A PAIN IN THE NECK.

Q. What is Dracula's favorite song?
A. PEG OF MY HEART.

Conclusion

The party ideas in this chapter have been designed with younger children in mind, but there's no reason to let them have *all* the fun. The next chapter contains Halloween party suggestions for older children, teenagers and adults.

ADULT HALLOWEEN PARTIES

Fortunately, Halloween is *not* just for children, and neither are Halloween parties. In fact, a Halloween party is a terrific excuse for adults to act like children, and have a lot of fun in the process.

The ideas and suggestions in this chapter can be used for both small Halloween parties and large affairs sponsored by organizations and other special-interest groups. We've included sections on invitations, party games, conducting a seance, spooky magic tricks, and refreshments. Halloween decorations are covered in chapter 7.

If you've never given a Halloween party before, or if you're looking for new ideas for your next one, read on!

Invitations

You can set the mood for your party before it even begins by designing unique and colorful invitations. Call your affair a Zombie Party, a Haunt-In, a Ghost Gathering, or just a Haunted House Party.

Your invitation might read: "Come park your broom at my house at the bewitching hour of _____. It'll be a scream . . . yours." Sign the invitation "Your Ghost Host." Make your invitations in the shape of miniature coffins, and invite guests to come pay their "last respects."

Get a left-handed friend to print your invitations backwards. Your guests, upon receiving the invitations, will have to hold them before a mirror to read them. Make sure to phone everyone later to make sure they read the invitations correctly!

If you want to give your guests a shock, try this idea. Bend a piece of wire in a U-shape, as in the illustration. Fasten a rubber band on each side of a small metal ring and attach this to the ends of the wire. Attach the wire to the letter with strong adhesive tape. Twist the ring until it becomes taut. Fold the invitation to hold it in place, and it is ready for mailing. When the invitation is removed from the envelope and opened, the noise will give your friends an unexpected shock.

Why not have a ghost write the invitation before your friend's eyes? First, squeeze some lemon juice into a small bowl. Use a small brush to paint your message on ordinary white paper. After the lemon juice has dried, print in ink "Hold this paper over a flame for a message from the spirit world." When held over a flame, the ghost writing will turn brown and mysteriously appear on the paper.

Mail your invitations at least three weeks in advance so your guests will have ample time to rent or make costumes. Mention on your invitations that everyone *must* come in masquerade. Remember, costumes make the party.

Games and Stunts

This section contains several ideas for games and other stunts that will keep your party lively and your guests entertained.

Aside from the fun they provide, games are an excellent way to get your guests circulating and meeting each other.

Try to keep the activities within a specific time period. Keep the party moving by leading your guests from one game to another. However, be flexible. If you see that your guests are enjoying themselves in a particular game, then stay with it.

Bobbing for apples is a traditional Halloween party game, and a lot of fun even for adults. Get a large basin, fill it with water and ice and make sure the apples have no stems. Have bathing caps and towels on hand for those who don't wish to get their hair or costumes wet. An interesting variation on apple-bobbing is the "apple exchange." Give a guest an apple and have him tuck it under his chin. Choose another guest (preferably of the opposite sex), and tell the first guest to transfer the apple from under his chin to under his partner's, while both keep their hands behind their backs. The gyrations that will follow are guaranteed to be a "scream."

Get several people involved with a Ouija board. As you are asking for a sign from the spirit world, have someone rap on the front door or turn the hose on the front window. This will startle your guests into momentarily believing in your psychic abilities.

No Halloween party would be complete without a story telling session. Spine-chilling ghost stories are terrific for creating the perfect party atmosphere. Turn out all lights except for a burning candle. The flickering flame of the candle, and the shadows it creates will give your guests chills. Have each guest tell a horror story or relate a personal haunting experience. You may want to read a classic short horror story aloud, such as "The Telltale Heart" by Edgar Allan Poe or "The Monkey's Paw" by William Wymark Jacobs.

You may wish to give out prizes for the best costume or to the winner of a party contest. If you have two winners, give them the "Gruesome Twosome" award. You could award such prizes as a Venus fly trap, a pack of tarot cards, a book of ghost stories or even a small magic set.

The spooky stunts that follow are perfect for a Halloween party, and require very little preparation and few props. You'll find that they'll leave your guests either mystified or shaking with laughter.

Supernatural Body Lifting

Five of your guests can participate in this amazing demonstration. First, have someone of average weight sit in an armless straight back chair. He should be told to cross his arms, sit up straight, and relax.

Each of the other four guests has to assume a specific position. The first places his first and second fingers under the right knee, while the second places his two fingers under the arm at the right shoulder. The third places his first two fingers under the left knee, and the fourth places his fingers under the arm at the left shoulder.

Tell all five guests to take three deep breaths in unison, as deeply as possible. On the third inhalation, give the command to "Lift." Everyone will be amazed as your guest is lifted from his chair by just the use of eight fingertips.

The Exhumed Corpse

Blindfold five people, telling them they will be examining the body of a corpse, and pass out the dead man's "parts" to your blindfolded guests. Substitute the following for the dismembered parts of the body:

Brains:	Cauliflower
Intestines:	Wet Spaghetti
Eyes:	Olives
Ears:	Dried Apricot
(?):	Peeled Banana

Have these "parts" in bowls and pass them to one person at a time, telling him what is supposed to be in each bowl. This stunt is guaranteed to give your guests a shiver.

The Invisible Hand

To present this effect properly, ask everyone to leave the room. You will call your guests back one at a time.

In a corner of this room have two chairs facing one another. Call a guest into the room and have him sit in the chair with his back towards the wall. Sit in the other chair and tell your guest that you are going to place your two fingers on his eyelids. (See illustration #1.)

As you are about to place the tips of your two index fingers on his eyelids, your guest will shut his eyes. As soon as his eyes are closed, extend the second finger of your left hand (forming a V) and place these two fingers on the person's eyelids. (See illustration #2.) The guest will think that he knows where both of your hands are, but in reality you will have a free right hand with which you can perform some ghostly antics. Tap the person on the shoulder, rub his hair, etc.

Remove both hands, and instantly resume your original position as illustrated in the first diagram. This demonstration will startle your guests as he realizes that you two are the only ones in that corner of the room.

Next, ask your guest to take a seat elsewhere in the room and invite another guest in. Repeat the demonstration. It doesn't matter if the first person sees how the trick is done. Since the purpose of this trick is just to have some fun, the laughs surely increase as each person sees his friends "visited" by the invisible hand.

Wing Wing Wing

This trick is more of a gag than a game, but it's fun neverthe-less. Ask for a volunteer, and announce that you're going to give him a test that is used as a part of Astronaut training.

Take a sturdy piece of paper, and cut and fold it as shown in the illustration. Ask your "trainee" to place his feet together, extend both arms, and extend his two first fingers. Place the paper on his fingers. Tell him to stare at the wall and to listen closely to your voice. Say that you are going to spell a word that has 4 letters, and that when you are finished spelling the word you want him to say it three times as fast as he can.

Slowly say "W," making weird hand gestures around the person's head and body, as if it were part of the test. Follow slowly with "I," "N" and "G", and then quickly say "GO!" The person will blurt out "Wing, wing, wing!"

You then calmly pick up the paper, and say "HELLWO!"

Tic-Tac-Toe

The last stunt is another gag that you can play, for example, on that person who didn't show up in a costume. You'll need a large piece of paper, a quarter, and a well-sharpened #2 pencil.

Tell this lucky guest that you are going to play tic-tac-toe with him, and that you are going to bet one dollar that he can't get three O's in a row. That is, of course, if he plays by your rules.

First, draw the criss-cross lines on the paper. (See the illustration.) Then, tell the person that he must take the quarter and hold it between his two first fingers. Starting at the top of his forehead, he must roll it straight down over his nose and down his face, and without looking drop it on the paper. If he gets three O's in a row (no matter what direction) he will win a dollar. Tell your guest that you are such a good sport you'll give him the first O. This is where the dirty work comes in. As you place the quarter in the center tic-tac-toe box, move the pencil around the quarter so that the graphite is left on the edges. Trace the quarter with the pencil several times.

Hand the person the quarter and tell him to do as you told him. What he does not realize is that as he rolls the quarter down, he is going to have graphite pencil lines running down his face.

As he drops the quarter say, "You were pretty close to this box, so I'm going to give it to you." Again, make several circles around the quarter, making sure you rub the lead against it. Ask your friend to try it again.

After several attempts, hand your guest a mirror and watch his expression when he sees the graphite lines on his face. At this point, you'd better be ready to make a quick getaway.

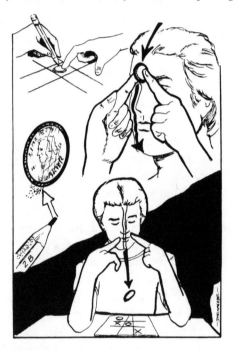

Ghost Arms

Ask a guest to stand in a doorway and place his arms at his sides. Tell him to put the back of his hands against the doorway and push, while you silently count to 60. Encourage the guest to push as *hard* as he can. Tell him when he's got 30 seconds to go, and count down from 10. When the minute is over, ask the person to relax his arms, and step out of the doorway. If he has followed your instructions, his arms will slowly rise into the air.

Spirit Seance

One of the highlights of your party could be a seance. A little preparation and rehearsal will have your guests believing that you have actually contacted the spirit world.

To present the seance you will need 2 school slates, a sheet of black construction paper, a bell, a horn, 4 aluminum pie plates, a squirt gun, 6 to 12 ping pong balls that have been painted with luminous paint, a card table and 4 chairs. You will also need the help of a secret assistant who will be willing to practice the seance stunts so they go off smoothly.

Begin the seance by announcing it in a ghostly tone of voice and asking for three volunteers. One of these must be your secret assistant. The four of you should then take your places at a card table, which must be placed near a light switch at one end of the room. Your back must be to the wall, and your assistant must be facing you with his back to the guests.

Before a single candle is lit and the room lights are turned off, gothic organ music or eerie sound effects should be playing in the background to set the proper mood. You are now ready to perform "spirit table lifting." (See illustration #1 and #1A.)

Instruct each person at the table to grab his left wrist with his right hand, and place the left hand flat upon the table. Then, tell the group that they will attempt to lift the table through "psychic energy."

While everyone places their left hands on the table, you and your secret helper extend your right forefingers beneath your left hand and under the edge of the table. The table can then be slowly lifted with your forefingers.

Next, conduct an experiment in "spirit slate writing." Two slates, blank on both sides, are placed together and a piece of chalk is placed on top of them. The slates are separated and a message has mysteriously appeared.

This stunt requires two black school slates, a piece of chalk, and a piece of black construction paper. The black paper should

be cut to fit inside the border of one of the slates. It should be loose enough to fall out when the slate is turned over.

Before the seance, write a message on one slate, cover it with the black paper, and leave both slates on the table. Show your trick slate first, front and back. As you are showing the second slate, tilt the first slate back and let the "insert" fall into your lap. (See illustration #2.) With a candle on the table and the other lights out, this move will go unnoticed. All that remains is to place the slates together, wait for several seconds, and "discover" the communication from the spirit world.

The last seance stunt will make your guests believe that a host of ghosts actually did manifest at the party. Have everyone at

the table change seats, and make sure that your secret helper is now sitting next to you.

Place the bell, horn, and aluminum pie plates on the card table, and instruct everyone at the table to hold each other by the wrist. Mention that this is necessary to prove that no one at the table is aiding the ghosts. Tell your guests that your are going to extinguish the candle and try to contact the spirit world.

When the candle is out, you and your secret helper release your grip on each other. (See illustration #3.) This will give both of you a free hand with which to carry out the spirit manifestations.

Either you or your secret helper can now reach on the table and sound the horn in the darkness. Next, one of you ring the bell while the other tosses the aluminum pie plates across the room.

For a real fright, remove the ping pong balls from your pocket. The balls must have been previously painted with luminous paint, and exposed to a bright light for several hours before the seance. Toss these "comets" around the party room. As your guests pick up these glowing objects and also toss them around the room, it will produce an eerie visual effect.

While this continues, your secret helper can remove the toy water pistol which has been filled with ice cold water from his pocket. He should squirt the water around the room at your guests, giving them cold, damp, spirit kisses.

At a given signal, your helper should place the water pistol back in his pocket. You should both join hands, announce that the seance has ended, and turn on the house lights.

Spooky Magic

How would you like to perform a mystifying magic show for your guests? This section contains 5 magic tricks that are both simple and effective. All that is required is a little bit of practice and a few props. And remember, a good magician never gives away his secrets.

Telephone Telepathy

Have one of your guests pick a playing card from a deck. Tell him that you know an omniscient magician, known as the Ghostmaster, who is also a master of extra-sensory perception. The Ghostmaster, amazingly, will be able to identify the card over the phone.

Dial the Ghostmaster's number and say, "Hello. Is this the Ghostmaster?" (Pause.) "Can I speak to him please?" (Pause.) "Here he is"—and you hand the phone to your guest. The Ghostmaster, in an eerie voice, tells the guest what card he is holding!

This trick requires a secret helper to play the Ghostmaster. As soon as you call your helper, and he hears you say, "Hello, is this the Ghostmaster?" he begins to recite the suits: spades, clubs, etc. As soon as he identifies the suit of your guest's card, you break in and say, "Can I speak to him please?" Now the Ghostmaster starts listing the card numbers: deuce, three, four, five, six, etc. When he gets to the correct card, you cut him off, turn to your guest saying, "Here he is . . ." Your guest says hello, the Ghostmaster tells him the correct card, and hangs up.

Magic Ashes

Prior to this trick, take a piece of moistened soap and write the number 1089 on your arm. Allow it to dry and roll down your

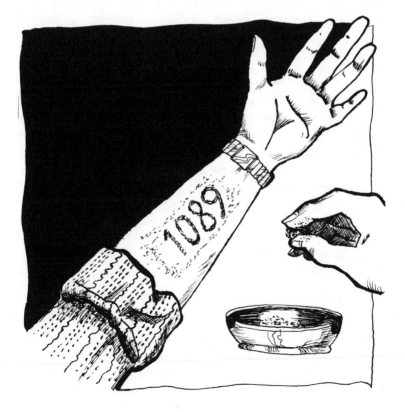

sleeve. Ask a guest to write a 3 digit number on a piece of paper. You then tell your guest to reverse the numbers and write them underneath. Substract the smaller number from the larger, reverse the difference, and add. For example:

$$\begin{array}{r} 945 \\ -\ 549 \\ \hline 396 \\ +\ 693 \\ \hline 1089 \end{array}$$

If this formula is followed the answer will *always* be 1089, providing consecutive digits are not used. You, the magician, have not seen any of the numbers. When the formula is completed, tell your guest to fold the paper and give it to you. You then burn the paper, roll up your sleeve, and rub the paper's ashes on your arm, as in the illustration. The ash will adhere to the soap, manifesting the magic "1089!"

How To Stop Your Pulse

Here's a quick effect that will demonstrate your power over your own body. Announce to your guests that you have the power to stop your pulse. Have one of your guests take your pulse, counting the number of beats in a minute. Then, in a dramatic voice, command your pulse to stop. Wait a few seconds, and ask someone to take your pulse again. You won't have one!

The secret: before the trick, roll a handkerchief into a lump and place it under your left arm, keeping your arm close against your side. When you want to stop your pulse, press your arm tightly to your side. The pressure from the handkerchief will stop the blood from going to your hand, and momentarily stop your pulse.

Hypnosis

You can use the power of suggestion to make your guests think you've hypnotized them. Attach a ring to a piece of string. Hand it to one of your guests, and tell him to suspend it over his outstretched palm. Tell him to concentrate on your words,

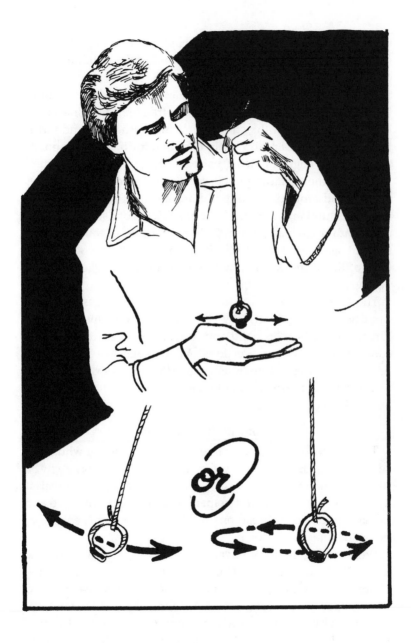

but to hold the string as steady as possible. Begin speaking the following "patter" to your guest: "Think of the pendulum of a clock, swinging, swaying back and forth, back and forth, back and forth. Now think of a line, a straight line, the line is getting longer, back and forth, straighter and straighter. Imagine a long line in the middle of the street, back and forth, back and forth. Follow that line, back and forth, back and forth." (At this point, the ring will begin to swing back and forth in a straight line!) "Now the line is starting to curve, it's going around in a circle, around and around, around and around. Just like a merry-go-round, around and around." (After a few seconds, the ring will settle into a circular pattern.) "Now the line is starting to go straight again, back and forth, back and forth." And so on. The path of the string will follow the direction you suggest in your "patter."

The secret is that, no matter how hard your guest tries, he can't hold his hand perfectly still—it will always move a little. The movements of his hand-and the ring- will be affected by his concentration on your directions. As you suggest a straight line or a circle, he will unconsciously cause the ring to sway that way. If it doesn't, it means he's not concentrating, or that you're not being persuasive enough.

Mindreading Miracle

This effect requires four or five participants, one of whom is a secret helper. Each person writes a thought—a color, a city, a number, a famous person, etc.—on a piece of paper and seals it in an envelope. Your secret helper writes a thought that you and he have previously agreed on, and when he seals his envelope, he bends one corner down.

When you get all the envelopes, hold up anyone *except* the one with the bent corner. Think hard, then say something like, "Someone is thinking of a number," or whatever else you and your helper have agreed upon. Ask whoever it is to stand up. Someone else may have written a number and will stand up too. If this is the case give the first figure of the number you know, and the other person will sit down. Slowly, as if it is a great strain, give the rest of the number. Your helper admits that, incredibly, you are right!

Now, tear open the envelope and take out the paper. This will be your next answer. Look at it and say, "Yes, the number was 455." Your helper nods and sits down.

Lay the envelope and paper down, and pick up another. Formulate a question that deals with the answer you *already* know from the previous paper, such as "Who is thinking of a flower?" When that person stands up, after a few tries tell him what he has written. Tear open the envelope (for the next answer), and "read" what is there. Lay the paper down, pick up the next envelope, and repeat the process.

Make sure to save your helper's envelope for last. Hold it up while giving the answer that was in the envelope before his. After you've torn it open, make sure you replace it at the bottom of the pile before you hold them all up at the finale of your performance, so that the envelopes will be in the correct order.

After this act, don't be surprised if your friends start to call you for the weather report!

Refreshments

No Halloween party is complete without some "specialty" refreshments, and listed below are some suggestions for deliciously different refreshment ideas.

Devilish Deviled Eggs

1 dozen eggs
½ teaspoon salt
2 tablespoons sweet pickle juice
1 tablespoon horseradish mustard
½ cup Mayonnaise

Hard-boil the eggs, cook, peel and cut them in half lengthwise. Remove yolks and mix with other ingredients. Refill the egg whites and sprinkle with paprika. Makes 24 halves. For a different twist, use sliced olives as a garnish on the eggs to suggest a disembodied eye.

Goblin Cupcakes

2 cups of all-purpose flower
1 tablespoon of baking powder
½ teaspoon salt
½ teaspoon vanilla
¼ cup shortening
⅔ cup sugar
¾ cup milk
1 egg

Sift the baking powder, flour, and salt together. Cream shortening and sugar together until fluffy. Add egg and mix thoroughly. Add sifted dry ingredients alternately with milk and beat thoroughly. Add vanilla. Pour contents into paper cupcake liners. Bake 15–20 minutes in 350° F oven. Makes 24 cupcakes. When cool, ice with orange frosting.

½ cup margarine or soft butter
1 tablespoon grated orange rind
1 egg
6 cups 10X sugar (sifted)
¼ cup orange juice

Cream butter. Beat in egg and orange rind, and gradually beat in 10 X sugar alternately with orange juice.

Jack-O'-Lantern Burgers

3 lbs. ground beef
1 package onion soup mix
½ cup water
salt and pepper to taste
12 slices of American Cheese
12 hamburger rolls

Mix the ground beef, onion soup mix and water together, and form 12 large patties. Broil or fry. While the burgers are cooking, cut jack-o'-lantern faces in each piece of cheese. Small triangles will represent the eyes and nose, and a larger wedge will form the mouth. Place the cheese mask on each burger so that the cheese melts slightly. Serves 12.

Punches

Two punch recipes are provided below, and here is a ghoulish suggestion for serving them.

Take several sterilized rubber gloves (a rubber surgical glove is ideal) and fill them with water and either red or green food coloring. Tie the end of the glove with a piece of string and freeze it.

After you have placed the punch bowl on the table, take one of the ice hands from the freezer. To remove the frozen ice hand from the glove, simply submerge the glove in lukewarm water and pull it off.

Now place the ice hand, palm up, in the bowl. If the hand should melt or become disfigured during the party, replace it with another fresh ice hand.

Witches Brew (Non-alcoholic)

3 cups water
3 cups sugar
3 cups orange juice
3 cups pineapple juice
3 cups lemonade
2 quarts ginger ale

Boil the water, and add the sugar until it dissolves. Add the remaining ingredients, except for the ginger ale, and chill. Add the giner ale when ready to serve.

Midnight Madness

12 oz. can frozen lemonade
6 oz. can frozen orange juice
1 large can of apricot juice
2 cups water
2 cups strong tea

1 qt. ginger ale
Vodka

Mix all ingredients except water, ginger ale, and vodka and chill. Add remaining ingredients when ready to serve. Vodka should be added to taste.

As a final, ghastly touch cut a large hole in the middle of an old card table or table leaf. Have a friend stick his head through the hole prior to anyone entering the room. A large cloth should be draped over the table so that your friend remains secretly hidden. A large dish cover should be placed over his head. Imagine the reaction when someone lifts the lid!

Conclusion

As your guests are leaving, don't forget to wish them "Pleasant Nightmares!" You can bet that they had a frightfully good time!

At the beginning of this book, we promised to show you how to haunt a house. The next chapter will do exactly that!

HOW TO HAUNT A HOUSE

As Halloween approaches, you may want to decorate your home in the ghostly spirit of the season, whether you are having a party or not. If you do plan a party, you can combine the ideas in this chapter with those in chapters 5 and 6 to create a spooky atmosphere for your guests. But, you may want to turn your home into a haunted house for the sheer fun of it, and perhaps invite your friends, neighbors and, of course, the trick-or-treaters, to take an eerie "tour." You'll find the decoration and special-effects ideas in this chapter to be easy to follow, and the materials needed inexpensive and readily available.

Decorations

The first step in "haunting" your house is to create a spooky atmosphere outside, especially if you have a good-size lawn, yard or porch. The yard can be turned into a cemetery by placing several cardboard tombstones painted with day-glow paint on the ground. An ultraviolet light hiding behind a tree can cast a chilling glow on the "stones" when the sun goes down. The names of friends and neighbors could be written on the tombstones.

Dig a hole the size of a grave and have the tombstone's inscription reading: "It's empty . . . but not for long." Have a pile of dirt and a shovel next to the grave marker. Make sure that the fresh grave is not too deep, and be sure to keep if off to the side so that no one accidently falls in.

Dig a shallow ditch in the walkway, place several old pillows or cushions in it, and cover them with dirt. When your guests arrive and step on the path, it will feel as if they are walking into quicksand.

Hang a cloth dummy from an upstairs window and have several dummies on the porch sitting in rocking chairs. If you have an intercom system, place one of the speakers on the porch, and have a recorded voice welcome your guests as they arrive.

A headless man or ghost could greet your guests at the front door, saying in a weird voice "Greetings, I am your M.C., otherwise known as the Master of Cemeteries."

Inside, cover the furniture with white sheets to give the house that "unlived-in" look. This effect can be enhanced by soaping windows to create a spooky film. Silhouette figures cut from black construction paper can be taped in the windows. Large

foot prints cut from white paper can be placed on the floor, up the walls, and across ceilings.

Carve several pumpkins and have these jack-o'-lanterns grinning from dark corners. Corn stalks can also be placed in several corners.

The traditional black and orange crepe paper streamers can be hung around doorways or across the corners of a room to the chandelier. Buy some large plastic skulls and cut the bottoms out. Set the skulls over the lights for a spooky chandelier, and for a really ghostly effect, substitute red light bulbs.

The walls of the house can appear "haunted" by hanging pictures or paintings upside down or on angles. You can also create an unusual effect with a wall clock. Wind the clock and remove the pendulum. This will cause the clock to "tick" faster and the hands to move more rapidly than normal. You and your guests will actually see time "fly."

Hang strips of aluminum foil from the ceiling. They will reflect any light source, and add to the other effects. The streamers can be kept moving by placing a small electric fan behind them.

Write ghoulish messages on the mirrors with red lip-stick. Try "Let me out!" or, "I'm trapped on the other side!" backwards to add to the confusion.

One of the best "spook" effects is to hang several rows of black thread in the doorways. The thread dangles down and brushes across your guests' faces, to create a feeling of spider webs. Make sure that the lights are dim so that the thread can't be easily seen.

Spider webs can also be made out of string and hung in the corners of a room. They should be painted with bright day-glow paint. An ultraviolet light will make the spider webs glow. Tie a few hangsmen's nooses and scatter them throughout the house.

Place several buckets of dry ice in different rooms to give the appearance of fog pouring in from the streets. Hot water must be poured on the dry ice and changed frequently to sustain the effect of a ground-covering mist.

You can buy weird-looking rubber masks and grotesque hands from the local costume shop. Have the fake hands sticking out of a vase or a piano, or attach a fake hand onto a light switch or doorknob. Imagine the reaction when someone reaches for one of these and finds another hand already there. A fake head or mask could also be sticking out of an attic door.

Buy a pair of inflatable fake legs and have these protruding from under a sofa. Rubber bats, fake spiders, plastic skulls, realistic snakes, chattering teeth, and pooh cushions can be placed around the house and under sofa pillows. Your budget and imagination are the only limits to the unearthly atmosphere that can be created.

Now that you've decorated your haunted house, let's look at some of the tricks that you can play on those who have enough nerve to come inside.

Spooky Stunts

If you really want to scare the wits out of your guests, arrange one corner of a room as a funeral parlor, complete with flowers and an open casket. A fake coffin can be easily made out of large sheets of cardboard. Place an accomplice in the casket wearing a scary false face. When one of your guests pay his "last respects," have the accomplice jump up from the coffin and let out a blood-curdling scream.

Hang a cloth-made dummy or luminous skeleton on the back door of the bathroom. When someone enters and shuts the door behind him, imagine his surprise when he finds he is not "alone." Better yet, hide one of your intercom speakers in the bathroom. When someone goes inside, count to ten and then say "I see you."

For a real thriller, send in a plague of worms to crawl through a room. Get several rubber worms from a fishing tackle shop, and tie them in 3 foot intervals to a thin line from a fishing rod. Before your guests arrive, feed the line out into the room, keeping the line close to a wall or furniture to prevent people from tripping over it. The worms should be hidden either under a curtain or a table. Your fishing rod is in the next room with the fishing line hooked onto it.

At the proper moment, reel in the worms. This effect will play havoc on your guests as they watch the squirming worms slither by them, especially if the worms have been coated with luminous paint and the room is dark.

Dress an accomplice as a scarecrow, and stand him in a corner before the guests arrive. Place several chairs in front of him, and instruct him to stand perfectly still. At the right moment, have your scarecrow put his straw arms around the group of people sitting in front of him.

Though tricky, it's possible to rig a tape recorder to one of the doors upstairs. Have the sound effects of a party on this tape. This tape will play for sometime until someone's curiosity causes him to open the door. As soon as the door is opened, the music and talking should stop. When he shuts the door, the party sound will continue.

Another tape recorder stunt is to record the sound of a thunderstorm. Have a flashing light in the hallway leading upstairs. The sound of a thunderstorm and the flashes of light will chill those who dare to ascend the steps.

Imagine blood dripping from the ceiling in your haunted house! All that is required is one bottle of theatrical stage blood, a piece of thin plastic tubing, a basin, and a cooking syringe (bulb). Fill the bulb and tube with as much stage blood as they will hold. Hook the tube to a pipe in the house or through a ceiling panel. A helper pumps on this bulb, forcing the "fake" blood out a drop at a time. The basin underneath catches the blood. You may find it more practical for the blood to drip into a bathtub or sink.

Buy several vibrating hand buzzers from your local novelty store. After winding the buzzers properly, scatter them on chairs throughout the house. Make sure the flat part of the buzzer is placed down. To hide them, cover the seats of the chairs with lightweight seat mats. Imagine the "shock" when someone sits on the chair and gets a surprising jolt.

By now your guests should really be in the mood for ghostly illusions. The next section outlines 13 different "special effects" that you can create.

13 Ghosts

No haunted house would be complete without real "live" (or dead) ghosts, and this section provides 13 ways to create these unearthly visitors in your home. While some of these methods are simple, others are quite elaborate and require preparations. You should use these stunts sporadically throughout your house to create the atmosphere you desire. (Some of these tricks and illusions would be ideal for a party seance. See chapter 6.)

Most of the items needed to produce spirits can be bought at hardware or department stores. Some of the ghost illusions, however, require luminous paint. If your local hardware store or hobby shop does not carry this item, it can be mail ordered. A list of dealers has been provided in the back of this book.

There are several important details to remember about producing manifestations. Effective background music will enhance the appearance of any horrible haunt you produce. If a "ghost" is coated with luminous paint, expose it to a strong light for several hours prior to its appearance. Also, remember that a luminous ghost will require either total darkness, or a semi-lit room. Finally, test your ghost ahead of time to insure that it works smoothly.

Disembodied Spirits

Just about any "ghostly" activity can be duplicated with the use of strong black thread. Doors can be made to open, pictures to fall from walls, chandeliers to sway, chairs to "walk" across the room, and books to drop from shelves. A button can be hooked to the end of each thread to make it easier to find.

Frightening Apparitions

Here is an easy method for producing a specter in your haunted house. As a guest walks down the hallway, he will see a phantom-like face appear, and then unexplainably vanish, right before his eyes.

The secret involves a mirror. Place a mirror on a 45-degree angle in a corner of a hallway or corridor, so that you see both your face and the face of anyone approaching. For this effect to work properly, the area should be as dark as possible. Study the illustration.

As a person approaches the mirror, shine a flashlight on *your* face. When your guest looks at the mirror, your ghostly reflection will appear. To vanish, simply turn off the flashlight and exit through another room.

Foreboding Skeleton

To create this apparition you will need a cardboard skeleton that has been treated on one side with luminous paint. Luminous skeletons are easily available at department stores, card shops, or novelty stores. Cover the side of the skeleton that is *not* luminous with wall paper or paint that is identical to that of the room to be used.

Next, insert small screw eyes into opposite walls near the ceiling. Run a piece of strong black thread up the side of one wall through the first screw eye, across the room through the second screw eye, and back down the other wall. The thread should be tied to either a tack or a small nail on both sides of the wall.

Place the skeleton with the luminous side facing one of the walls so that the skeleton is flush against it. This should go unnoticed in a semi-lit room, since the side of the skeleton that is covered with wall paper or paint should blend into the wall.

Finally, hook the skeleton to the thread so that it can be pulled away from the wall and travel across the room. It is now up to you and your secret helper to control the movements of the haunted skeleton while the lights are off.

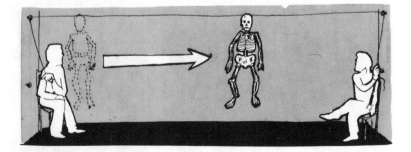

Green Grinning Ghosts

More macabre effects can be achieved through the use of luminous make-up, which is available at most costume shops. Apply the make-up to several of your ghostly helpers and at the right moment turn out the lights. The painted faces will shine in the dark like grinning ghosts. This make-up can also be applied to hands and fingers, so that when the lights are out, these ghastly hands will appear in the dark, float around, and tap your guests on their shoulders. The illusion of the glowing faces and waving hands will vanish when the lights are turned on.

Floating Heads in the Basement

This hideous apparition requires several yards of black cloth (either corduroy, velvet, or velveteen) and three 25-watt red light bulbs with reflectors facing the audience.

Cover one end of the wall in a large room with sheets of black cloth. Also cover the windows so there is no trace of light. Next, take the black material and make two ponchos. These will be placed over two friends, covering their entire bodies except their heads.

Place the three red lights about six feet in front of the curtain; these will be the only lights in the room. Your two helpers will be performing between the three red lights and the black curtain. Since this effect demands that it be viewed from a distance, a section of the room should be appropriately roped off so the illusion is not ruined.

This effect creates an astonishing feeling of the unreal. Your guests will witness two human heads without bodies hovering in mid air.

Ghost-Infested Room

Here is another method for conjuring elusive spirits and unseen ghosts.

You will need several dozen balloons and a balloon bag, which are used by large dance groups. Suspended from the ceiling, the bag will cascade balloons upon your guests when a rip cord is pulled.

If you can not find a balloon bag through a supplier of party goods or through a dance group, one can be made out of two large sheets of plastic. Take the sheets and secure one side of each to the ceiling so that they are parallel. The free ends of the hanging sheets should overlap when they are raised to the ceiling. Punch holes in both plastic sheets. To keep them together, run a piece of cord through the holes, weaving the cord through the holes in the sheets. The cord should be tied to wall and hidden so that no one releases it too soon. Next, fill the plastic sheets with balloons.

When the room is dark and the time is right, release the balloons. At first your guests will be surprised. After they realize what has happened, however, they will have fun laughing in the dark knocking the balloons about the room.

Vampire Bats

Luminous paint always produces eerie effects, and the next is no exception. A glowing bat will instantly appear in a pitch dark room, then flutter about before vanishing.

This trick is as simple as it is effective. All one needs is a cheap oriental fan. Department stores will carry them, if there isn't one lying about the house. Paint an image of a bat on the fan with luminous paint, and expose it for several hours to a strong light before the effect is to be created. Immediately prior to the manifestation, fold the fan up and place it in your coat pocket. In a dark room the fan can be taken from your pocket, opened, and waved in an up and down motion to create the bizarre image of a glowing bat fluttering about the room.

Portable Ghost

At your command, a ghost will appear in the center of a room, float about, then suddenly vanish.

This effect requires two 12-inch rulers and two pieces of black material, 2 by 4 feet. Paint the image of a ghost on one side of the black material with luminous paint. After the paint has dried, sew the second piece of black material onto the back of the ghost. (This is to prevent the painted image from seeping through to the other side.) Along the two foot edge, at the top, attach the two rulers end to end.

Expose the ghost to a brilliant light for several hours. When you are ready to put the spirit in operation, fold it in half lengthwise, roll it up, and place it in your pocket. All that remains is to unroll the material and wave the ghost about in the dark room.

Galloping Ghost

You may want to have a ghost haunting the outside of your house, as well as the inside.

To create this illusion tie a long piece of black elastic string onto the end of a long pole. Next, roll a towel into a bundle and place it in the middle of a large square of cheese cloth, or some other light material. Picking up the four corners of the square material and tying the elastic string immediately above the towel will form the image of a ghost.

At the proper moment, stick the pole out of an upstairs window and wave it about. The cloth, animated by the weight of the towel and the elastic, will appear to be a galloping ghost.

The Uninvited Guests

During the evening, when the lights are out, a ghost materializes in a most uncanny manner. It wavers, floats about, then suddenly vanishes towards the ceiling.

This creepy spook is nothing more than a rolled-up window blind. First cover the windows to block out any trace of light. Then hang a window blind with a painted luminous figure of a ghost on the side of the shade that will be facing the room. Expose the ghost to a bright light, and roll it up just prior to the arrival of your guests. Simply pulling the blind down in a dark room creates a wonderfully hair-raising effect.

Spectral Phenomena

This next stunt is supernatural enough to fool and horrify anyone who sees it. In the dark, a glob of light appears to hover in mid air. This vaporous light pulsates like an amoeba, and then expands as it floats through the air.

You will need an old umbrella. It is best to use a standard umbrella rather than one that opens automatically. After remo - ving the covering from the hinged ribs, attach small round cardboard circles to the center and the ends of the rods. Next, coat the circles with luminous paint.

After the circles have been exposed properly to a light source, the umbrella can be hidden anywhere in the house. When the lights are out, grab the umbrella by the handle and wave it slowly around the room. Opening and closing the umbrella will make the circles of light seem to multiply, for a truly startling effect.

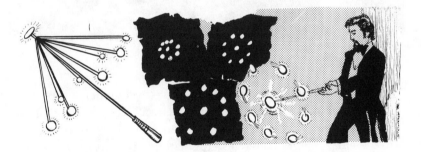

Ethereal Forms

This effect is rather complicated, but it is well worth the effort. When the lights are turned out, a horde of unearthly phantoms, shrouds, and peering ghosts rise in the air and then suddenly vanish.

This illusion requires a roll of black material at least 36 inches wide. The longer the material, the more spooks you can produce. Use luminous paint to draw ghosts and ectoplasmic forms on the long ribbon of black material. Fold the cloth in an accordion fashion, and place the material in a deep box.

Just before the lights are turned out, place the box near a pipe or rod that has been securely attached to the ceiling. There should also be a dark curtain hanging from the pipe. When the lights are turned off, remove the black material with the ghosts from the box and feed it over the pipe behind the curtain. Stepping behind the curtain, slowly pull the material towards you. It will look as if an endless procession of disjointed zombies, hobgoblins, and spirit enigmas are rising from the damp earth and vanishing into the mist of the heavens.

Wandering Skeleton

While all the lights are out, a headless skeleton suddenly appears in the middle of the room. After it has walked about and performed a few crazy antics, the lights are turned back on, and—to the amazement of all—the supernatural visitor is nowhere to be found.

You will need a helper to accomplish this effect. Get an old suit from a second-hand clothing store. On the back of the suit, using luminous paint, paint a skeleton: the skeleton's legs and pelvis on the pants, rib cage, arms, and neck on the coat.

Expose the "skeleton suit" to a strong light for several hours. After your friend has put on the suit, he should nonchalantly walk into the room, keeping his back towards the wall, away from the other guests. At a precise moment, turn out all the lights. Your secret helper shoud now turn his back *towards* the people and stroll through the room. It will appear as if a gruesome skeleton is searching for its head. The skeleton can vanish by simply mingling with the other guests as the lights are turned back on.

Conclusion

While haunting a house is fun, it can also be profitable. Every Halloween, clubs and service groups raise much-needed funds with paid admissions to haunted houses which their members design and operate. You've seen how easy and inexpensive it can be to create a ghostly mansion. The next chapter will show you how to have your Halloween fun and fatten up your organization's treasury at the same time.

Photo courtesy of *The Baltimore Sunpapers*.

HALLOWEEN FUND-RAISING PROJECTS

Halloween is the perfect opportunity for a club, school or church group, recreation council, or other service organization to conduct a fund-raising activity. This chapter includes ideas for fund-raising haunted houses, indoor and outdoor Halloween festivals, a Halloween dance, and a pumpkin contest.

Planning and the enthusiasm of all of an organization's members are the two key elements for a successful Halloween fund-raiser. Preparations for the projects discussed in this chapter have to begin weeks and, in some cases, months before Halloween. It is a good idea to appoint a committee headed by a strong leader to identify and assign the work that needs to be done. Each and every member must make a significant contribution, based on his or her talents. Local businesses should also be canvassed for donations, in exchange for free advertising at the event.

If an organization is not experienced at conducting a fund-raiser, it's best to keep the event small and uncomplicated. In later years, the effort can be improved and expanded. Also make sure that the event is publicized. Handbills and posters are the cheapest method, but some TV and radio stations offer free advertising to community groups. It never hurts to ask.

The next section deals with the most elaborate—and most lucrative—Halloween fund-raiser: the Haunted House.

Fund-Raising Haunted Houses

A fund-raising haunted house is a major project requiring a great deal of planning and hard work. For some organizations, conducting a haunted house is the *only* fund-raising event, and members work on the project all year long. Why? Because not only is it a lot of fun, but it is possible to generate thousands of dollars in admission fees and concessions.

Getting Started

The first thing needed, of course, is the "house" itself. This can be an old building or barn, or the basement of a church or school; any large space can be temporarily converted by constructing a maze from plywood, cloth, paint, rope and cardboard. Two sample mazes are shown on the next page.

It is best to have just one entrance to the house but several exits should be provided, even if they are hidden, in case of an emergency. There must be adequate parking nearby, especially if an old house or barn out in the country is being used. Also, make sure to allow adequate room for those waiting in line to enter. If people have to wait outside, decorate the grounds like a cemetery, as described in chapter 7.

Many different skills are needed to plan, build and run a successful haunted house. The key element is a committee chairman who has the ability to get things done on schedule, and to manage the work of others. Besides the chairman, members will have to fill the following jobs:

Advertising director—takes care of flyers, newspapers, and TV
    and radio coverage.
Concessionaires—to cook food and take care of the stands.
Painters, electricians and carpenters—to build the maze, etc.
Parking lot attendants—6–8 people with flashlights who guide
    people into the parking areas.
Security personnel—several volunteer policemen.
Crowd controllers—4–5 people who dress up as monsters, ghouls,

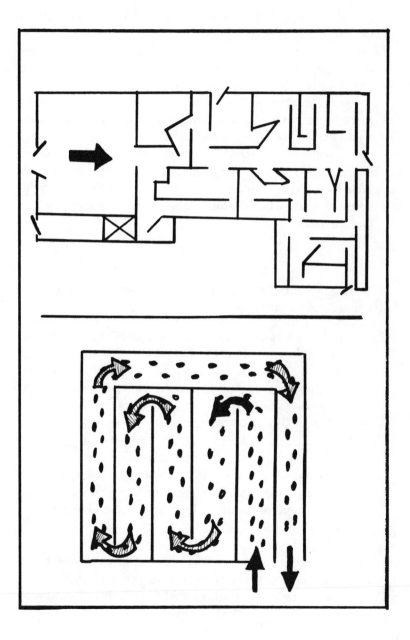

etc. and roam throughout the haunted house to make certain nothing is out of line.

Roaming Ghouls—2–3 ghouls or gorillas who sneak up on patrons outside the haunted house, or on the parking lot, to set the mood for things that are about to follow.

Stationary characters—depending on the number of characters in the rooms of the haunted house or involved in the playlettes, twice that many will be needed. A monster's job is a tiring one, and the characters will need to be relieved at least hourly.

Tour guides—8–10 monster guides, who travel in sets of two, are needed. One monster leads a group of people through the haunted house while the other tails along to make sure no one is left behind.

Decorating the House

The decoration ideas in Chapter 7, of course, can be used. Here are some additional suggestions.

Lighting: Use an assortment of various colored light bulbs and special lighting equipment such as strobe lights. It is also effective to use ultraviolet lights to cast an eerie glow on day-glow paint. A dimmer switch could be used with the ultraviolet light to create other ghostly effects. Green lights can also be used to create a spooky atmosphere.

Eerie Music and Sound Effects: These are a must for any haunted house. Try using an eerie musical background or sound effects such as moans, groans, heartbeats, cat cries, rolling thunder and howling banshees. Other noises such as piercing whistles, fog horns, sirens and sudden loud noises should be set off at infrequent intervals.

Other Effects: Long pieces of black thread should be attached inside dimly lit rooms so that they hang down and brush against people's faces. In dark corridors, firmly attach 12" pieces of black tubing to the walls so that they protrude and brush against spectators legs and ankles.

Safety First

Although its's fun being scared and scaring others, don't let anyone get carried away, and be sure there are no safety hazards in the house itself. Here are a few safety tips.

- At the entrance to the haunted house, display a sign which lists the safety rules such as: "No smoking, no food or beverages, no one under 6 allowed, etc." Enforce the rules strictly.

- Don't overcrowd the house, and keep all exits clear. Make sure the tour guides know where the exits are, and that they keep the groups moving.

- Make sure that none of the monsters or other ghouls touches anyone, especially from behind.

- Frequent safety inspections should be made of all lighting and other electrical fixtures.

- Keep the passageways clear of wires or anything else that can be a hazard. If the haunted house has stairs, be sure they are visible.

- Have several fire extinguishers available.

- At the end of the night, make certain that all electric lights, etc., have been unplugged.

Above all, use common sense and make sure the patrons do the same.

Conducting Tours

Groups of 8–10 people are met at the door by a tour guide, dressed as a witch or some other spooky character. As the group is led through the haunted house, they encounter wandering ghouls and monsters, some of whom menace them and others who simply ignore them. It's a good idea to place dressed-up mannekins around to add to the confusion. Eerie music is playing, lights are flashing, and screams are heard. As the group goes from room to room, they witness short skits, lasting from

30 to 90 seconds, depicting some horrible event. After each of these playlettes, the group moves to the next room, and finally to the exit. As they leave, they are congratulated for having "survived" and move to an area where concessions are offered for sale.

Haunted House Playlettes

Below are some suggestions for 30 to 90 second skits to be presented. Each is relatively easy to design and produce.

The Gorilla Escapes

As the lights are turned up, the group sees a hairy gorilla inside a large cage. A mad doctor enters the lab and gives the gorilla an injection with a needle. When the doctor leaves, the ape begins to pound on his chest and rattle the bars to the cage. A strobe light goes on. Two of the black bars of the cage are made of thick rubber tubing. The ape bends the bars to the cage, escapes, and heads slowly toward the group. They are quickly led to the next room.

The Mummy's Curse

Inside an Egyptian temple, the group sees an upright mummy case. An archeologist opens the case and it is shown to be empty (the case has a fake back to it leading to another area which conceals an assistant dressed up in a mummy costume). As soon as the archeologist shuts the door to the case, the mummy immediately comes out and dramatically strangles him. Several other assistants, also dressed as mummies, sneak into the room through a hidden door behind the group. As the group tries to get away from the approaching mummy, they are confronted by an entire group of mummies, advancing slowly towards them. The guide orders everyone to move immediately to the next room.

No Bones About It

Inside the next room several ultraviolet lights are connected to dimmer switches. As the lights are turned up the group sees two skeletons sitting inside a cemetery, using a tombstone as a makeshift table. One skeleton begins to pour the other a drink from a large tea pot. Both skeletons raise their cups toward the audience, announce "Cheers," and begin to drink as the lights fade out. The skeleton suits, tombstones, tea pot and cups must be painted in colored day-glow paint in order to be visible under the ultraviolet light when it is turned up. Other areas inside this room should be painted with flat black paint.

The Phantom

At the next room, patrons hear organ music and see the back of the Phantom of the Opera, seated at an organ. Either a real organ or recorded music can be used. The organist plays a haunting musical melody for about one minute and then stops and slowly turns around and faces the group. A strobe light goes on as the phantom's horrifying face appears. As he slowly rises, the group hurries on.

Frankenstein and Igor

As the group is led to the next room, they see an operating table with Frankenstein's monster lying upon it. A hunchbacked character enters the laboratory, and turns on a jacob ladder device. The group hears the sounds of thunder and sees flashes of lightning. Slowly, Frankenstein's monster lifts himself off the table, and heads toward the audience. Igor quickly grabs two realistic long rubber snakes and makes a hissing noise as he shakes the snakes toward the group.

Giant Spiders

At the next scene, the group sees a shimmering aluminum foil curtain. As the music gets louder, a 1 foot high spider slowly creeps out from the curtain and heads back inside. At another side of this curtain another spider repeats the action of the first. Next, very quickly, both spiders are thrust at the group's feet. The spiders can be made from paper-maché, wire and fur. They are attached to long black poles, and strategically placed so that they can be pushed out toward the group, but not close enough to be touched.

The possibilities are endless. It's always effective to dramatize a scene from a movie with which everyone will be familar. Be sure, though, to change the scenarios from year to year so that people will want to keep returning for another tour.

Advertising

Publicity and advertising are vital to the success of any fundraising event, and this is especially true of a haunted house. No matter how good a haunted house is, it will fail unless the community knows about it.

Organizations should designate one of their members to be the advertising director. This person is responsible for producing and distributing flyers and posters. An example of an advertising poster is shown on page 152.

Flyers can be distributed any place where large numbers of people gather such as supermarkets, schools and shopping centers. Make certain that permission is obtained from the proper authorities first. An organization might also try offering a scout troup free admission to the haunted house providing they distribute circulars in the community.

Radio and TV stations will sometimes offer free advertising to non-profit organizations. In addition, most city and community newspapers will even send reporters and photographers. It is best to contact newspapers personally to generate more of a response. Be prepared with advertising materials such as photographs and other information as to where the haunted house is located, the admission price, the operating hours, etc.

Just because a haunted house is successful one year does not guarantee success for the next. Advertising needs to be continued and expanded from year to year if a haunted house is to continue to be profitable.

Final Notes

It is a good idea to have a dress rehearsal for a haunted house before it opens for business. Several groups should be led through the house to insure that all is running smoothly and safely. If an organization has never run a haunted house, it's a good idea for the planning committee members to visit several of them before they attempt their own.

Haunted houses should run anywhere from 11 to 20 days, and end on Halloween night. Reasonable hours are from 7 to 10 or 11 on weekdays, and 7 to 11 or 12 on Friday and Saturday, depending on the crowds. Be sure that extra workers are on hand to staff the haunted house on weekends and other peak nights—especially on Halloween.

For further information on this subject, obtain a copy of *How to Operate a Financially Successful Haunted House* by Philip Morris and Dennis Phillips. This book is available through costume and magic shops, or can be obtained from the suppliers listed in the back of this book.

Non-profit organizations can also purchase copies of *The Great Halloween Book* in quantity at substantial discounts for resale as a fund raiser. For more information, contact Liberty Publishing Company, Fund Raising Division, Post Office Box 298, Cockeysville, MD 21030.

Halloween Festivals

A Halloween festival is really an indoor carnival with a Halloween motif. This event is ideal for an organization which has its own large hall, or has free access to one. In general, the hall is decorated appropriately and admission is charged to enter. Concessions can be sold, and other attractions such as carnival type booths could be offered. Some ideas for booths are:

Fortune tellers
Horoscopes and astrology readings
Halloween grab bags
Weight guessing
Handwriting analysis
Caricature sketches

Continuous movies and/or puppet shows could be shown for children, and games such as those described in chapters 5 and 6 could be played. If there is space, a "mini" haunted house could be set up, with admission charged.

It is important that a public address system be available, and that all events are properly supervised by adults. Since all of the workers will be organization members, there's very little overhead involved with conducting the festival. Ideally, a Halloween festival should run several nights with a special event—such as a raffle drawing or a magic show—offered on Halloween night.

Halloween Dances

Masquerade balls have always been popular events, and many organizations capitalize on that popularity to raise funds by holding a Halloween dance. People enjoy dressing up in costumes and masks to go to a dance—maybe it is because this is probably the one chance they have all year to assume a secret identity.

The key elements in planning a Halloween dance are advertising, decorating the hall (and renting one if the organization does not have its own), booking a dance band, organizing refreshments and concessions and, most important, selling tickets. Each organization member must work hard to sell tickets if the dance is to be a success. Some organizations raise additional revenue by selling raffle tickets for a prize to be awarded at the dance.

It's not a good idea to *require* costumes at a Halloween dance—some people don't like to dress up, and this may keep them away. But be sure to mention in the advertising that prizes will be awarded for various costume categories—funniest, scariest, most original, etc. A panel of judges will select the winners and award prizes during one of the band breaks. If possible, recruit a local celebrity to announce the winners.

The hall can be decorated using some of the ideas in Chapter 7. In addition to decorations, some organization members could dress up as fortune tellers and offer their services from table to table. If the budget permits, a magician could be hired to perform a brief magic show at a band break—one with lots of audience participation.

All of these elements—music, decorations, concessions—must be geared to the personality of the organization's community. But if properly planned, a Halloween dance can become a strong annual fundraiser, guaranteed to generate revenue for years to come.

Outdoor Halloween Festivals

An organization which has access to a large enclosed outdoor area should consider sponsoring an outdoor Halloween festival. The festival should be held on several successive nights in case rain or other bad weather occurs one or more nights. In any case, an admission fee is charged to patrons attending the festival, and other concessions can be offered inside.

Publicity is the key. Every available medium should be used—radio and TV (if provided as a public service), posters, flyers and newspaper articles. Schools, churches and other agencies can help spread the word.

The festival attractions should be spread through the grounds to keep the crowd distributed over the entire area. A public address system is also a must, both for emergency announcements and to draw attention to various attractions and special events. It is also important to alert police officials to the festival, so that adequate security can be provided.

Attractions must be planned with all age groups in mind; especially for high school teenagers, since one of the purposes of a planned Halloween event is to keep that particular group from getting into trouble. Some activities should also be designed for very young children. Listed below are some ideas for Halloween festival attractions.

- Music, either piped over the PA system or provided by live bands. School bands are a good resource, since they will perform free of charge.
- Strolling entertainers such as clowns and magicians could mingle with the crowd to provide impromptu entertainment. Wandering "monsters" are also a good idea.

- A costume contest could be held, judged by a panel of local celebrities. (See the next section for ideas on how to stage a pumpkin contest.)

- Outdoor games such as tug-of-wars, pie-eating contests, or ducking for apples could be played.

- Concession booths could sell apple cider, popcorn balls, candy apples and other Halloween treats. Arts and crafts could also be displayed and sold.

- A community sing-a-long, led by a local celebrity, could be featured.

- A Halloween bonfire could be lit and left to burn through the evening. Make sure to check with local fire officials to insure adequate supervision for this event.

Finally, the festival could conclude with a ghost story session read over the PA system, accompanied by some sort of live enactment. For example, one organization re-enacts the Legend of Sleepy Hollow. Lights are dimmed and a 10 minute condensation of the story, complete with pre-recorded music and sound effects, is told. At the end of the story the sound of hoofbeats is heard, and a headless man clad all in black rides along the edge of the crowd carrying a pumpkin in his hand. After he rides off into the darkness, a fireworks display is shot off to end the evening.

As long as the area to hold the festival is loaned with no charge and all of the organization's members freely donate their time to the effort, an outdoor Halloween festival can be a relatively uncomplicated way for an organization to make money and provide a service to the community as well.

Pumpkin Contests

A Halloween pumpkin contest requires little or no investment and, if properly supported by the local media, can be extremely lucrative. The basic idea is to accept entry fees from contestants and to display the pumpkins in a hall or enclosed outdoor area which would be open to the public for a modest admission fee. Of course, a pumpkin contest could also be an activity at a Halloween dance, festival, or even a Haunted House.

The first step for a non-profit or charitable organization is to approach a local radio or TV station with the idea. These stations usually try to emphasize their "public service image" through sponsorship of such events, and the organization should be able to secure free advertising and/or air time to promote the contest. It is ideal if the station offers its facilities to display the pumpkins, and agrees to have local media celebrities attend. The stations must be approached weeks or even months before Halloween, so that the project can be properly planned and promotions scheduled.

Handbills can be distributed and posters placed in store windows. As contestants pay the entry fee and submit their pumpkins, the pumpkins are displayed according to the category in which they've been entered—funniest, most original, scariest, etc. Cash or other prizes will be awarded to the winners in each category.

A small admission fee is charged to view the entries. Patrons submit votes for their favorite pumpkins; these votes will determine the winners. Refreshments—pumpkin pies, for example—can be sold, as well as other concessions. A face painting stand could be set up, where some of the artistic members of the organization could paint small pumpkins and other Halloween decorations on children's faces with several colors of make-up.

The night before Halloween is the best time to close the contest, although the exhibit could remain open through Halloween night. At that time, the winners could be announced, prizes awarded, and your organization goes home with the profits.

THE GREAT PUMPKIN

A grinning jack-o'-lantern is the universal symbol of Hallow-een, but did you know that turnips instead of pumpkins were originally used? Did you also know that the goop inside a pump-kin (which you've always thrown away before carving your jack-o'-lantern) can be used to make delicious foods?

This chapter celebrates the "great" pumpkin. It traces the history of the jack-o'-lantern, and offers a few tips on pumpkin carving. There are also suggestions for variations on the tradi-tional jack-o'-lantern, and, finally a section of recipes that use fresh pumpkins to make everything from pie to soup.

The First Jack-O'-Lantern

According to Irish legend, a long time ago there lived a miser named Stingy Jack. One Halloween, Jack invited the Devil to have a drink with him. He also persuaded the Devil to change himself into a gold coin to pay the innkeeper. But, as soon as the Devil did so Jack popped the coin into his pocket. Because Jack had a silver cross in the same pocket, the Devil could not change himself back, since the cross robbed him of his evil powers. Jack made the Devil promise never to claim his soul before he finally let him go.

After a long and sinful life, Jack died. He was turned back from the gates of Heaven, and made his way to Hell. But he couldn't enter hell either because of the Devil's promise to him. The Devil angrily threw a glowing coal at Jack, who quickly hollowed out a turnip and put the coal inside to light his way. Jack has been wandering through the darkness as a lost soul ever since, holding his lantern before him.

The legend of Stingy Jack spread to England and Scotland, where people believed that a lit jack-o'-lantern protected them from Jack and the other restless spirits that roamed the earth on Halloween. Grotesque faces were carved on the hollow turnips to frighten the spirits away, and each house had its glowing jack-o'-lantern by the front door on Halloween night.

When Irish and Scotch immigrants came to America in the 1800s, they brought the traditions of Halloween with them. They discovered that pumpkins made perfect jack-o'-lanterns, and began to use them instead of turnips. The tradition spread throughout the country and has lasted to this day.

Carving A Jack-O'-Lantern

You'll need:

A pumpkin (of course!)	Sharp thin knive
Newspaper	Small candle
Long-handled spoon	Small pie plate
Bowl	Matches
Black magic marker	

Cover the work surface with several layers of newspaper sheets. Use the knife to carefully cut a circular lid in the top of the pumpkin. Be sure to cut the top on a *slant* with the knife point toward the center. This will prevent the top from falling into the pumpkin later.

Let's stop right here. Everyone *knows* that small children should not handle knives, but every year thousands of them are cut while carving jack-o'-lanterns. It happens so often that there is a formal medical name for it—Pumpkin Carver's Little Finger Syndrome (no kidding!) So, no matter how hard your child or little brother or sister begs to help with the carving, do them a favor and refuse. And don't forget to be careful yourself.

After you have cut off the lid, set it aside and scoop the pulp and seeds out with the spoon, and put this mixture into the bowl. Here's something for the younger children to do! It's a good idea to save the pulp and seeds, because fresh pumpkin is delicious when correctly prepared.

Use the magic marker to outline the jack-o'-lantern's features. You are limited only by your imagination, but don't make the features too intricate.

As each feature is cut out, reach inside the pumpkin and with your finger push out the cut piece.

Light the candle and pour a small drip of wax onto the pie plate. Next, stick the candle to the plate, and set the plate inside the pumpkin.

When you are ready to display your jack-o'-lantern, light the candle and replace the lid.

Other Pumpkin Ideas

An interesting jack-o'-lantern variation is to remove the *bottom* of the pumpkin instead of the top. This makes it easier to attach and light the candle; you simply remove the entire pumpkin shell, and replace it when the candle is lit.

While it is still daylight on Halloween, place your jack-o'-lantern outside. Remove the candle and replace it with a small can of hot water. Drop a piece of dry ice into the water, and an

eerie mist will begin to flow out of the pumpkin. Be careful with the dry ice—it's best to use a towel or gloves to handle it.

If candles make you nervous, a small flashlight can be substituted. Use a green or red bulb in the flashlight for a spooky effect.

A different type of jack-o'-lantern is the sculptured pumpkin. Outline your design (a grotesque face, a skull, etc.) with a crayon on the rind. Lightly trace the design with a sharp knife. Peel away the outer rind in thin layers, and complete the carving. Use watercolor paints to make the carved features stand out boldly. Add hats, hair, etc. to complete the sculpture.

Pumpkin Recipes

American Indian tribes were growing and eating pumpkins centuries before Columbus reached the New World. When the colonists arrived in the early Seventeenth Century, they quickly discovered that cooked pumpkin was delicious when used in soup, pies, bread and other foods. Pumpkins were later found to be a good source of vitamins A and C, especially when used fresh.

So, if you've saved the pulp and seeds from your jack-o'-lantern, we've included some recipes that use fresh pumpkin. Remember too that the pulp can be frozen and used later, for possibly a Thanksgiving pumpkin pie.

Pumpkin Seeds

Wash and drain the seeds. Pour ¼ cup vegetable oil on a large cookie sheet. Spread seeds on the sheet, coating them well with oil.

Bake in oven at 350° until seeds are lightly brown (8–10 minutes). Remove, drain on paper towel, and sprinkle with salt. Store seeds in an air-tight jar until used.

Pumpkin Pie

¾ cup brown sugar
1½ cups fresh pumpkin
½ teaspoon salt
3 tablespoons melted margarine
1 teaspoon cinnamon
½ teaspoon nutmeg
3 eggs
¾ cup milk

Separate eggs and lay the whites aside. Combine the yolks and all other ingredients in a large bowl and mix well. Fold in the egg whites and mix well. Spoon mixture into a 9″ unbaked pie shell. Bake at 350° for one hour, or until a knife inserted in the center comes out cleanly.

Pumpkin Bread

1¾ cups all-purpose flour
1½ cups sugar
¾ teaspoon salt
1 teaspoon soda
½ teaspoon ground cinnamon
½ teaspoon ground nutmeg
½ cup vegetable oil
2 large eggs
⅓ cup water
1 cup fresh pumpkin
½ cup chopped walnuts or pecans

Combine all dry ingredients in a large bowl and mix well. Combine pumpkin, water, eggs and oil and mix well. Add dry ingredients slowly and beat thoroughly. Stir in nuts and pour batter into greased loaf pan. Bake at 350° for 75–80 minutes. Cool 15 minutes before removing from pan. Makes 1 9″ by 3″ by 5″ loaf.

Pumpkin Squares

2 dozen graham crackers (crushed)
1½ cups sugar
½ cup margarine
5 eggs
1 -8 oz. pkg. cream cheese
½ teaspoon salt
2 teaspoons cinnamon
1 envelope plain gelatine
¼ cup cold water
2 cups fresh pumpkin

Mix graham cracker crumbs, margarine and ⅓ cup sugar together, and pack in a 9" by 13" pan. Combine 2 eggs, ⅔ cup sugar and cream cheese, and beat until light and fluffy. Pour mixture over graham crackers and bake for 20 minutes at 350°. Remove and cool.

Separate 3 eggs, combine the yolks, pumpkin, ½ cup sugar, salt and cinnamon in the top of a double boiler, and cook over boiling water for 5 minutes, stirring often. Remove from heat. Sprinkle gelatine over water in a small pan and stir over low heat until dissolved. Add to mixture in double boiler, and let cool. Beat egg whites until stiff. Fold into mixture, and pour over baked layers. Refrigerate and serve with whipped cream.

Pumpkin Soup

2 large onions, chopped
1 teaspoon curry powder
1 tablespoon salt
5 cups chicken broth
½ cup butter
4 cups half-and-half
4 cups fresh pumpkin

Saute onion in butter until tender. Sprinkle with curry powder and saute 2 more minutes. Remove and place in a large saucepan. Stir in pumpkin and salt. Add half-and-half, stirring constantly. Stir in broth. Cook over low heat, stirring occasionally. Serves 16.

SUPPLIERS

A.T. JONES & SONS, INC.
708 N. Howard Street, Baltimore, Maryland 21201
(301) 728-7087
Halloween Headquarters — suppliers of spider webs, horror masks and hands, make-up, books, capes, props and numerous Halloween accessories. Enclose two first class stamps for brochure.

MORRIS COSTUMES
3108 Monroe Road, Charlotte, North Carolina 28205
(704) 332-3304
Masks, novelty items and assorted Halloween accessories. Enclose $5.00 for large catalogue.

RUBIE'S COSTUME COMPANY
One Rubie Plaza, Richmond Hill, New York 11418
(718) 846-1008
Numerous costume accessories and prop items available. Enclose $3.00 for catalogue.

STROBLITE COMPANY, INC.
430 West 14th Street, New York, New York 10014
(212) 929-3778
Luminous paint, ultraviolet paint and special theatrical lights ideal for haunted houses. Free catalogue available.

The Great Halloween Book and *Creative Costumes* are published by Liberty Publishing Company, Inc. Both books are available in better bookstores nationally, or may be ordered directly from the publisher. Mail to Liberty Publishing Company, Inc., 440 South Federal Highway, Deerfield Beach, Florida 33441

Gentlemen:

Please rush the following order to the address noted below. Enclosed is my check for $_____ which includes the retail price of the title(s) noted plus $2.00 for shipping and handling.

_____copies of *The Great Halloween Book* ($7.95 each)
_____copies of *Creative Costumes* ($5.95 each)

Ship to:

Name _____

Address _____

City _____ Zip _____

ACKNOWLEDGEMENTS

This book would not have been possible without the tireless help of many friends and some of my colleagues in the magic world. Specifically, I would like to thank:

A.T. Jones and Sons Costumers, Inc., for their invaluable assistance with the costume and make-up chapters; Larry Subotich, Cindy Lee and Scott Walker who modeled for costumes and make-up; Photographers Laura Drogoul, Joe Hinkleman, Alfred Eris and Paul Hutchins; Anthony Corradetti, make-up artist; Nick DiMarino, Chairman of the Gray-Charles Recreation Council; Bill Steinacker, magical illustrator; and fellow magicians Sid Lorraine from Canada and Jeffery Atkins from England.

Finally, I would like to acknowledge three special individuals:

Jeffrey Little of the Liberty Publishing Company for his guidance and direction; George Goebel, renowned magical illusionist, for his creative help throughout the text; and Dan McCarthy for his guidance in the post-operational work and for serving as editorial consultant.

Mark Walker

INDEX